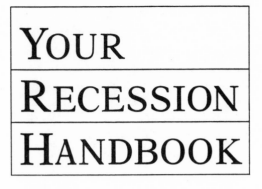

YOUR
RECESSION
HANDBOOK

YOUR RECESSION HANDBOOK

HOW TO THRIVE AND PROFIT IN HARD TIMES

Stephen M. Pollan
and Mark Levine

WILLIAM MORROW AND COMPANY, INC.
NEW YORK

It is the policy of William Morrow and Company, Inc., and its imprints and affiliates, recognizing the importance of preserving what has been written, to print the books we publish on acid-free paper, and we exert our best efforts to that end.

Library of Congress Cataloging-in-Publication Data

Pollan, Stephen M.
    Your recession handbook : by Stephen M. Pollan and Mark Levine.
        p.   cm.
    ISBN 0-688-10855-5
    1. Finance, Personal. 2. Recessions. I. Levine, Mark, 1958–
HG179.P55545   1991
332.024′02—dc20
                                                                        91-562
                                                                        CIP

Printed in the United States of America

First Edition

1   2   3   4   5   6   7   8   9   10

BOOK DESIGN BY NICOLA MAZZELLA

ACKNOWLEDGMENTS

The authors would like to thank the following individuals for their insight and advice: Gary Ambrose and Norman Dawidowicz of Personal Capital Management Inc., Joel Arron and Carl Gimber of Right Associates; Bill Davidson of Marine Midland Bank; Richard Kimball of Eagle Capital Management; Tim Kochis and Steve Roullac of Deloitte & Touche; Larry Lewis; Ed Moldt of the Wharton School of Business at the University of Pennsylvania; Frank Palma of Goodrich & Wells; Nelson Rosabal of CNBC; Stuart Rosenblum, JD, CPA; Ed Scanlon of NBC; Lawrence Stern of National Reprographics Inc.; and Kenny Tillman of S&S Sound City.

We'd also like to thank Shannon Carney, John Duffy, Hillary Kayle, Stuart Krichevsky, Karen Loscalzo, Jane Morrow, Gregor Roy, Mark Solomon, and Doug Stumpf for their support and assistance.

And most of all we wish to express our heartfelt love and gratitude to Corky Pollan and Deirdre Levine for their encouragement, patience, and understanding.

CONTENTS

1. How to Stop Worrying and Start Taking Charge   11

Part I: Digging In
2. Renewing Your Employment Vows   19
3. Making Your Business Lean and Mean   35
4. Checking Your Financial Foundations   55
5. Trimming Debt and Establishing a Cash Reserve   73
6. Cutting Your Income Tax Bill   89

Part II: Fighting for Your Life
7. Appealing a Layoff and Negotiating Severance   99
8. Dealing with Unemployment   117
9. Surviving Financial Emergencies   135
10. Pulling Up Stakes   149

Part III: Going on the Offensive
11. Getting Reemployed Quickly   169
12. Buying the Home of Your Dreams   189
13. Investing Your Money Wisely   201
14. Starting Your Own Company   217
15. Expanding Your Business   231
16. Renovating Your Home   239
17. Buying a Vacation or Weekend Home   253
18. Buying Undeveloped Real Estate   261

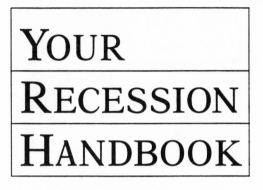

YOUR
RECESSION
HANDBOOK

CHAPTER 1

How to Stop Worrying and Start Taking Charge

When one door closes,
fortune will usually open another.
—Fernando de Rojas

There's a palpable fear in America, a sense that the economy has ground to a halt and is starting to slide downhill. In the morning you pick up the newspaper and read about another round of massive layoffs at the factory outside of town. On the way to work you pass the beautiful Victorian on the corner that's been up for sale for more than six months. You arrive at the office and find a memo from the corporation's chief financial officer stating your department's budget has been halved while sales quotas have been doubled. Once you return home, you discover your twenty-nine-year-old son, with his possessions in tow, waiting in the driveway. He blurts out something about having lost his job and being unable to pay rent, before asking if he can move back in. After the excitement of the surprise family reunion passes, you flip on the evening news and hear that another major bank has failed, a famed insurance company is foundering, and Standard & Poors has downgraded the rating on a nearby city's

municipal bonds. You don't need an economist to tell
you something is wrong.

This recession has shaken some of your fundamental beliefs. You used to think all banks were safe places
for money. Now you realize the FDIC is no guarantee
of solvency or security. You used to assume insurance
companies were impregnable bulwarks of capitalism.
Now even they appear vulnerable. You used to believe
your income would go up each year. Now you're just
worried about holding on to your job. You used to rely
on your home going up in value every year. Now you
find its value has dropped more than 15 percent in the
past five years.

How did all this happen and who's to blame?
Some point the finger at the environmental movement
for putting shackles on technological development.
Others say it's the fault of the Federal Reserve Board
for worrying too much about inflation and not lowering interest rates quickly enough. A few blame the
bankers for their hesitancy to lend, and the bank regulators for making them so reticent. And many feel it's
all Saddam Hussein's fault, saying his invasion of Ku-
wait sent the price of oil soaring and pushed the already fragile economy over the edge. Years from now,
when economists and historians look back on the recession of 1991, I believe they'll find the answer was much
simpler: As a nation we fell prey to the siren call of
easy money.

Credit really is a wonderful device—it lets you
take a bite of the apple while you still have teeth. But,
as the 1980s proved, it's also a dangerous drug, more
exhilarating and addictive than cocaine. The more we
borrowed, the more lenders offered us. Why save to
buy something with cash when you could use plastic
and have it today? Executives of large corporations
asked much the same question. Realizing that if they

paid a high enough rate of interest, they could bring out the latent greed in commercial and investment bankers, they issued scores of junk bonds. It's as if the whole nation—government, business, and consumers—went on a decade-long spending spree, and now the bills have arrived and we can't afford to pay them.

Instinctively we've stopped buying, making the economy even worse. Let me explain: The economy is like a spiral that can spin either up or down. Consumer confidence is the gear that decides the direction in which the economy spins. When consumers are confident about the future, they buy things. In response, retailers buy from wholesalers to stock their shelves for the hungry consumers. The wholesalers turn around and buy more from the manufacturers, who hire more workers to fill the orders. These workers are also consumers, and with their new jobs they, too, become confident—and the spiral continues.

But what happens when consumers realize they've borrowed too much money, think their banks and insurers aren't safe, realize their jobs aren't secure, and find their homes are dropping in value? They become frightened, lose confidence, and stop buying. That means retailers stop buying from wholesalers, who in turn stop buying from manufacturers, who in response lay off workers. When they hear about the layoffs, consumers lose even more confidence, and the spiral continues, but this time, downward.

Rather than doing something to break out of this descending spiral, most Americans seem paralyzed. Things were so easy for us in the 1980s that we became lazy—it's human nature to do only as much as we need to get by. We entered the 1980s lean and trim athletes in the game of life, getting to work early, paying close attention to our investments, and watching where our money went. As we became successful, we lost our edge, putting on some extra pounds, slowing down, growing complacent. Now the economy has started spiraling down rather than up, and we're not in shape to do all the things we need to do. Instead of addressing the problem head-on we're hiding under the blankets, hoping it all goes away. We're living in the problem rather than in the solution.

This book will change all that. It shakes you out of your lethargy and gets you started once again. It cuts through all the alternating reports of gloom and hope the media has been reflexively broadcasting with each shift in the stock market. It offers clarity, explaining that the only true economic indicators are the cash in your pocket and the balances of your bank accounts. It lights a path past the obstacles and problems and illuminates the opportunities that lie along the road to recovery.

It examines your fears, helps determine if they're valid, and, if they are, gives some advice on protecting yourself. The secret to dispelling anxiety is understanding. Once you understand what, if anything, you must worry about, you'll have something tangible to hold on to. Fears of recession will no longer be mysterious phantoms—they'll become tangible obstacles that can be overcome. This book offers strategies and tactics for dealing with any emergencies that you couldn't prevent from happening. And then it immediately puts you on the offensive, seeking out opportunities to exploit the recession and further your financial and career goals. Caught up in fear, few realize a recession is the best time in the economic cycle to: review your savings-and-investment plan; buy the home of your dreams; buy a second home; buy vacant land; renovate your current home; start your own business; buy someone else's business; and expand your existing business.

This program of taking charge of your life and

working your way out of the recession is the same simple, practical process I've been passing on to all my clients for the past year. It wasn't derived from theoretical analysis but from practical experience—my own.

I was frightened by the recession just as you are now. All the mistakes you made, I made as well. I began my present consulting practice in 1978, after years as an attorney, banker, and venture capitalist. The business was a child of the 1980s, and so was I. I preached the joys and magic of leverage and real estate, and being a true believer, I went even farther than my clients. As my practice expanded and I became more successful, I spent less time in the office and paid less attention to details. My staff grew and my expenses soared. Suddenly I woke up to what was happening. I started playing out worst-case scenarios in my head. Fear began clouding my vision and judgment. I calculated how much I had "lost" in real estate because my property went down in value. I became worried about my retirement planning—even though I've no intention to ever stop working. I was worrying about the future, rather than dealing with the here and now. I began doubting myself.

But then I remembered that whenever you're in doubt, go back to the fundamentals. That's exactly what I did. I retraced my steps back through the decade and found where I took a misstep, where I veered from the fundamental path. Once I knew what I had done wrong, I stopped projecting what potential long-term problems I'd face and began dealing with short-term issues. What do I need to do today? I asked myself. Then I just started putting one foot in front of the other. I gave up trying to steer and row simultaneously. I just concentrated on rowing, realizing the steering would take care of itself.

In the process of working myself out of my recession-induced malaise, I came to a remarkable realization: This economic downturn is actually a golden opportunity for all of us. I firmly believe that whenever one door closes, another opens. While the door to the 1980s era of prosperity based on easy leverage has closed, the door to a new era of prosperity based on quality and service has opened. But right now we find ourselves in a long, dark hallway between the two doors—the recession. In wending our way down the hallway, overcoming obstacles as we go, we shed excess baggage, sharpen dormant skills, and acquire new talents. By the time we reach the next open door, we'll be in top condition, in better shape than we've ever been before, fully ready to take advantage of all that lies ahead. The recession can be a time of personal renaissance for all of us, regardless of age, location, or career, as long as we are willing to take charge of our financial lives.

Have no fear: This recession is only a temporary adjustment in the economy. The economy didn't fall sick overnight, and we won't wake up one morning and find it's cured—but it will recover. Region by region, industry by industry, the economy will turn around. But before we can plan to take advantage of the inevitable shift in the economy, we need to get past those obstacles in the hallway. The first is the threat of losing our job, and with it our stream of income. Overcoming this hurdle is the subject of chapter 2.

PART I
DIGGING IN

Defense, however, is of much more importance than opulence.
—Adam Smith

CHAPTER 2

Renewing Your Employment Vows

By the work one knows the workman.
—Jean de La Fontaine

When times are tough, the first people to feel it are employees. That's a simple fact, not a dose of extremist propaganda. Most American businesses, rightly or wrongly, have always chosen layoffs as their primary method of dealing with economic downturns. If widgets aren't selling, the board of Acme Widget decides to lay off some of the people down at the plant or in the main office. In some industries there have been continual rounds of layoffs throughout the 1980s. But thanks to the perceived economic prosperity of the 1980s, those of us who weren't in stagnant industries—who weren't, for example, working on assembly lines in Flint or Lackawanna—could remain secure in the notion our jobs were safe. Rather than getting nervous about the reports on the evening news of massive layoffs in the auto industry, we looked at the pictures and decided maybe it was time to buy a new television.

But with the economy in this downhill slide, it's clear none of us are safe anymore. There once was a widely accepted belief that there was an unwritten, un-spoken contract between management and employees stipulating that workers would keep their positions as long as they did their work. This belief has been shattered. Corporate executives whose employees make great widgets but who bought into the junk-bond funded-leveraged buyout mania of the 1980s, are trying to salvage their own inflated salaries and perquisites—which more than tripled in the past decade—by cutting their labor costs. Companies losing market share are responding to competitive pressures by firing workers, not top managers. Business caught in the recessionary vice of soaring costs and plummeting revenues are trimming worker payroll rather than executive salaries. All across America, in almost every industry, companies—both large and small—are laying off their employees in response to the recession.

And it's not only blue-collar workers who are receiving pink slips. For the past ten years management gurus and economic pundits have been preaching the benefits of "down sizing." They proclaim that by streamlining organizational structures, businesses improve the quality of products or services. While the intent of these experts is to prod American business toward more efficient operations, many executives take this talk as an open invitation to lay off their middle managers. Rather than fire the fellow who runs the photocopying machine—who's probably making minimum wage—corporate managers are giving the ax to their account executives, salespeople, and department managers—thus trimming more from the payroll—and eventually firing the photocopy clerk anyway. Even employees of service businesses, which were once thought to be immune to recessions, are being laid off.

While the traditional rule of "last hired, first fired," is still being observed by some organizations, most now reject seniority as the sole basis for deciding who goes and who stays. Top executives get together with their number crunchers and human resources experts and determine who's "adding value" to the company's products, services, sales, or operations. It's no longer enough simply to "do your job." The average employee might be safe when the economy is booming, but in a recession the only ones who can feel secure are those clearly above average. Not all those people being laid off are bad workers. The vast majority in fact do their jobs efficiently—but today efficiency just isn't good enough.

"Employee value" may sound like a logical or even clinical way of making the termination decision, but it's still not objective. Productivity may be part of the equation, but so are demeanor and appearance. More than anything else, whether or not you're adding value to a company or business is a subjective decision based on the perception of your immediate supervisor.

You may have been the apple of your supervisor's eye when you started on the job, but you could well have slacked off a bit as time went on. During those first few months you were the personification of energy and enthusiasm; you were dressed for success; you smiled and had a pleasant word to say to everyone. In those early days you staked out your own territory, sought out responsibility, and offered suggestions and opinions. But after a few months you changed. It didn't happen overnight, but bit by bit the enthusiasm and excitement drained out of you.

Don't feel bad about this: It's human nature for the automatic pilot to kick in eventually and for behavior and performance to become humdrum and predictable. Maybe it started the morning you got up late, threw on some clothes that didn't match too well, and no one seemed to notice the difference. Or perhaps it all began when you had a suggestion but chose not to mention it, since your boss had rejected all your other ideas up to now. The added spark you brought to the organization as a newcomer was probably snuffed out once you began to feel secure in your ability to get the job done and comfortable with your role in the organization. In other words you got complacent.

Now, with a recession here, the personnel department has stocked up on blank pink slips, and management is on the lookout for complacent employees. You can make sure your name doesn't end up on one of those slips by actively reviving the spark you had when you first joined the company, making sure your employer's perception of you is positive.

The first step in renewing your job vows is to spend more time in front of the mirror each morning. It goes without saying that your grooming should be impeccable, and your garb clean and pressed. But the message you convey through your personal appearance should also be carefully examined and appropriately modified. Rule number one is to forget about making fashion statements, at least until the recession is over. Your fish necktie or papier-mâché parrot earrings may have been cute at other times—but they probably don't match your employer's image of the model employee.

What exactly is that image? It's easy to figure out: Just look at how your boss dresses. If he doesn't have a beard or mustache, then shave yours. If she only wears suits and simple gold-stud earrings, do likewise. Your supervisors should look at you and see a reflection of themselves. But don't be so blatant in your emulation that the two of you look like identical twins—that's overt obsequiousness and will probably backfire. Simply duplicate the essential elements of your supervisor's style—for example, match a solid-colored business suit with a solid-colored business suit. You want the effect to be subliminal. Suddenly your employer sees you in a slightly different, even more

flattering, light. If your shift to a more corporate en-
semble does spark any comments or questions, simply
shrug and say, "I came to realize that I'm actually
more comfortable when I'm dressed this way."

Don't stop paying attention to your appearance
once you arrive at the office. Make sure to check your
hair and makeup several times: once during midmorn-
ing, right after lunch, and again a couple of hours before quitting time. Keep a toothbrush, a tube of
toothpaste, some dental floss, and a small bottle of
mouthwash in your desk drawer. After lunch spend a
couple of minutes on oral hygiene. If you've a heavy
beard, bring an electric razor to the office and shave
sometime during the afternoon. Refrain from rolling
up your sleeves, kicking off your shoes, or loosening
your tie, unless perhaps the air-conditioning breaks
down or you're asked to do some heavy lifting. It's
okay to remove your jacket when in your own office,
but the moment you step outside your personal space,
the jacket should go back on. Every time you're in public during the business day, make sure you look as
fresh and clean as you did when you walked in that
same morning.

The most important thing you can wear is a smile.
It may sound ridiculous, but it's true. Employees who
smile and are cheerful have a good chance of still being
on the job long after the mopes have been sent packing.
Smiling conveys enthusiasm and satisfaction and im-
plies loyalty. It signals you're a positive force in the
company. One of the first people let go is the company
sourpuss.

I know what you're thinking: All this talk of attire
and expression is a bit superficial. Your supervisor
wouldn't decide whom to lay off based on what he
wears or how often she combs her hair or brushes her
teeth. Well, maybe. But your appearance contributes

a great deal—perhaps more than you realize—to your supervisor's overall perception of you as a person and an employee.

Your appearance and manner create what's called a halo effect. If you look like a good employee, subconsciously your boss perceives you're a good employee. In effect your appearance casts a halo over the rest of your persona. The reverse is also true. Dress slovenly or frown all the time and your supervisor perceives you as a sloppy and disgruntled employee. And once they get an idea in their heads, either positively or negatively, supervisors look for evidence to back up their feeling.

That's why only positive things should distinguish you from your peers. Stop taking an active part in company gossip sessions. Don't sling mud along with everyone else. Certainly listen to what's being said—it can be invaluable information—but don't participate. If you've nothing nice to say, say nothing. If pressed for an opinion, find something positive to say, even if it appears you're damning them with faint praise. Noncommittal statements like "he's certainly very experienced" can get you off the hook without having to stick a knife in someone else's back. When the company cuts overtime or your boss announces there will be no bonuses, don't get involved in the inevitable behind-the-scenes protests. If asked for your opinion, just say something like "The company's health should really be our number-one priority." Make no mistake about it: If it comes to choosing which of two equally able employees gets laid off, the one who smiles, who gets along with everyone, and who's better dressed wins out every time.

This isn't selling out, it's survival. While not impossible, finding a new job in a recession is very difficult, as you'll see in chapter 11. Sure, principles are important, and you should never compromise your ideals when it comes to freedom of speech and religion, or ethnic, racial, or gender equality. But you must be prudent at the same time. Would you rather give up the fish tie or your job? Where you draw the line is a matter of personal conscience. However, during this recession you may want to draw the line in pencil, not pen. It's a war out there, and if you must become a guerilla, disguising yourself in the uniform of the other side, so be it.

Another outstanding way to stand out positively is to work longer hours—show up early and stay late. In this recession the workaholic is making a comeback. All you heard in the 1980s from human-resources experts was that workaholism was indicative of inefficient time management. Top managers and executives, who tend to be obsessive themselves, never really agreed. They think that those who work longer hours are more productive. Remember, being productive equals adding value to the company, and adding value to the company equals keeping your job. Supervisors also equate time with commitment. They have a tendency to prowl the halls before and after hours. Your stock rises immeasurably when your supervisor sees you still at your post after everyone else has headed home. Similarly, being at your desk bright and early marks you as enthusiastic and conscientious.

I learned this lesson well when I worked as a real estate analyst for a major bank. When I arrived at 9:00 A.M. on my first day at the job, my assistant—a veteran employee—warned me the bank president had a habit of making a complete tour of the executive offices every morning at 8:00 A.M. and every afternoon at 6:00 P.M., looking to see who was hard at work and who wasn't. From that day on I stopped looking at the clock on the wall and instead used the bank president as my time keeper. I made sure I was at my desk when he made his morning and afternoon inspections. He never directly mentioned my diligence, but I knew from the smile on his face when he saw me hard at work, that my long hours were appreciated.

One excellent way to fill up those extra hours at work is to do some reading about your company and industry. When we're out in the job market, we think nothing of spending hours at the library investigating the goals and strategies of companies that we're interested in. But once hired, most of us stop seeking out objective information about our organization or industry and instead rely on company propaganda and rumors. Preinterview research marked you as a hot job candidate; on-the-job research, especially during a recession, marks you as an astute, concerned employee. Keep up-to-date on changes taking place in your industry, and your company's response to those changes. Become familiar with the company's product lines and technologies. You need not be a technical wizard, just an informed and interested worker. Once you've absorbed this information, you'll find your knowledge manifests itself automatically, so there's no need to run around the company dropping technical phrases. Another benefit to all this study is it can help you plot a survival strategy.

Scour newspapers, trade journals, and internal literature for information on the goal or mission of your company. Try to find out where the company is heading and how it intends to get there. Pay particular attention to anything you discover about company's priorities. Is your firm going to be stressing customer service in the future? Does your company's chief executive officer seem to be using the word *quality* in every speech she delivers? Whatever the case, you want to make sure you fit in with the company's stated goals and plans. If cost efficiency is the new company motto, then liberally add it to your on-the-job vocabulary. Think of how you can demonstrate to your supervisor that you're committed to this new creed; you're "with the program." Your goal is to show you fit into the company's future.

A good way to show you and the company are on the same wavelength is to initiate ideas and offer suggestions. For example, if customer service is the company's goal, suggest ways you, your peers, and your subordinates can speed up order processing or deliveries. Before suggesting anything, consider its costs. Paying careful attention to the bottom line is the one trait every owner or good manager loves in an employee. Regardless of your company's stated goal or mission, every supervisor is looking for ways to cut costs without affecting quality. Simply say to your supervisor, "I hope I'm not out of line, but I know you're really concerned with cost savings and I've come up with an idea. You may think it's silly . . ." Then pause as if waiting to be discouraged—don't worry, you won't be. "Well, I've discovered . . ." Just make sure your suggestions, and all other communication with your supervisor, is done in private.

Your suggestions and ideas should be as selfless as possible, indicating your concern with the company's well-being, not just your own. Don't feel every idea has to be a winner. Managers are more impressed with the fact that you care and have come up with something than whether your idea has or hasn't any merit.

In some cases your research may lead you to a frightening discovery. Let's say you work for Jim Bob's Pizzas Inc. and everything you've uncovered points toward the company moving away from direct sales—the branch you're in—and toward wholesale sales. First be grateful you found out about it early—it gives you an

opportunity to take some actions. You can begin pep-
pering your supervisor with ideas on how wholesale
sales could be improved through the use of some direct-sales techniques. Indicate you grasp the big
picture; you're not a direct-sales specialist but a sales-
person who happens to be doing direct sales. Start me-
andering over to the wholesale department and seeing
if they need any casual help. And while you're subtly
trying to shift your position, take your Rolodex home
one weekend and photocopy it so that you can start
looking for another job.

Regardless of what your company's goal or mission is, it's concerned with holding on to employees
who are personally responsible for either revenue production or cost efficiency. That's why the next step in
the process of renewing your vows with your employer
is to establish or solidify a power base. A power base
can be anything that indicates you're more than just a
cost to the company. Perhaps you've a stable of steady
customers whose loyalty is more toward you than the
company. You can subtly make sure your supervisor is
aware of this by asking your customers to write letters
on your behalf. Don't launch a whole direct-mail campaign—it looks suspicious. Instead, whenever your customers tell you how much they enjoy doing business
with you or how big a help you are to them, thank
them and ask that they express the sentiment to your
supervisor. Your efficiency or productivity can also
serve as a power base. If you run the most cost-effective department in the company, point this out to your
supervisor in an indirect manner. For example, suggest
that other departments institute a cost-saving technique you've been using.

If you don't have a power base, develop one right
away. Make your department the most productive or
efficient. Cultivate some personal loyalty from custom-

ers. A fast and effective way to build a power base is to become an expert. Select an aspect of your company's operations that falls within your realm of responsibilities and become the organization's authority on the topic. It can be anything from desktop-publishing software to discount airfares and accommodations—as long as you're the company guru, and your supervisor realizes it, it's a power base and helps solidify your job.

Another way to solidify or establish a power base is to broaden your responsibilities. Look for vacuums you can fill within the company. This can be particularly valuable for those who find themselves isolated in the company's more remote outposts, or stuck in a department that doesn't figure in future plans. Never assume another responsibility without first asking your supervisor. Leaping into a void uninvited smacks of opportunism. Besides, discussing the matter with your supervisor first gives you yet another opportunity to demonstrate your value. Break the ice by saying to your supervisor you hope you "aren't stepping on anyone's toes" but you've noticed, for example, there doesn't seem to be anyone specifically responsible for the company's trade-show exhibit. Explain you've "developed some shortcuts," or have "streamlined" your own department's operations and have an opportunity to take on additional work. Never bring up compensation, and if it's mentioned by your supervisor, stress that you weren't looking for more money, but were just trying to increase your own productivity. Whether or not your boss goes along with your suggestion, your initiative, selflessness, and concern for the organization mark you as a valued employee.

Vacuum filling worked wonders for one client of mine. A part-time television commentator, he saw the writing on the wall down at the station. Budgets were being trimmed, and there was a rumor the program he worked for was going to be trimmed from sixty to thirty minutes. He knew the first staff cuts would take place in on-air talent, since that's where the fat was. Rather than simply bemoan his fate, he began searching out other things he could do for the station, looking for other needs he could satisfy. He graciously and unconditionally offered his unique services to other programs. He began helping out in other areas as well, pitching public relations campaigns and offering to help promote the station in any way he could. Even though his program was eventually shortened, when his contract came up for renewal, rather than getting a pay cut, he actually got a raise.

While building up or broadening your power base, add to your skill base as well. There's a renewed reverence for continuing education among today's managers. Where once they viewed ongoing study as an indication that an employee was looking to get another job, now they see it as a statement of professionalism and dedication—as long as they aren't required to pay for it or give you time off. If your company offers training programs, take advantage of them. Pursue additional academic study as well. Financial specialists would do well to enroll in a marketing course or two. Marketers help their status by taking a finance class. If you work for an international company, learn to speak Japanese, or German, or Russian. Almost everyone would benefit from taking business-writing or legal courses. If you don't have a degree, work toward one. And if you do have a diploma, pursue a more advanced degree.

As with every other aspect of your renewing-vows campaign, it's important to subtly let your superior know of your actions. In the case of continuing education, the best technique is to ask your supervisor's advice. Explain to him or her that you've decided to take a course in finance, for example. Say, "While I'm comfortable preparing marketing plans for the company, I've realized a grounding in finance will give me a firmer grasp on the overall decision-making process." Never ask your supervisor if you should go back to school—it smacks of desperation and obvious supplication. Present the decision to take a finance course as a *fait accompli*, but ask for her advice on *which* finance course you should take. Even if your supervisor passes you along to personnel for the answer, you've once again demonstrated your value to her and the company.

By doing all these things—improving your appearance, expanding your hours, researching your company, offering suggestions, solidifying your power base, and broadening your skills—you've planted the seeds for renewing your job vows. The fertilizer that nourishes each seed and ensures that it bears fruit is a one-on-one conversation with your supervisor.

If you've a sane, stable, and confident employer, the meeting shouldn't present a problem. Make an appointment for a Tuesday, Wednesday, or Thursday, after lunch, but not too near quitting time. If your CEO comes in early in the morning, try politely ambushing her then. Take a direct, but cogenial approach. Say to her, "Ms. Martin, I wanted to tell you I really enjoy my job. I hope I'm not overstepping my bounds, but I just wanted to know if I'm on the right track with the company. I want to be a part of the team and I want to be sure I'm doing all I can." Ask what her goals are and what you can do to help accomplish them. Draw on all your research and demonstrate that you understand the big picture, that you're on board with the program, but that you need some reassurance and maybe some help in setting priorities. Such a humble, nonthreatening speech, delivered after planting all the other seeds, should just about ensure that your job is safe.

The only danger in having this discussion is that you might not get an entirely positive response. If your supervisor does express some concern about your performance or behavior, learning about it early at least gives you a chance to take corrective steps. Immediately acknowledge your boss's criticism and say, "I know. That's why I'm here today." Explain you've had a problem—a dispute, illness, or death in the family—that has caused you to be preoccupied. But go on to say that all that's over, the problem has been taken care of, and you're ready for a renaissance at work. By offering an explanation for your less-than-stellar performance you've shifted the focus from you to the problem itself. Stressing that the situation has been resolved gives you a grace period either to clean up your act even more or to find another job. If the conversation grows increasingly ominous, you should start shoring up your last lines of defense—turn to chapter 7, which describes what to do if you're fired.

Such a direct, frank discussion is impossible if your boss is either paranoid or incompetent. In those cases you must make an end run to personnel, while finding a way to endear yourself to the nut who's in control of your destiny. How do you endear yourself to someone who's fearful and paranoid? Try making a gift of your best ideas and suggestions. This is as simple as saying, "Wasn't it your idea that . . ." or "Didn't you once say to me . . ." If offering him bureaucratic gifts isn't enough, try something more tangible. Is your suspicious supervisor a baseball fan? Then present him with a couple of tickets to a game, saying, "I can't use these, but I thought you might like them." Where you draw the line on such behavior is up to you—but just remember: The bigger and more frequent the gifts, the more obvious and less effective they are; and no job is worth degrading yourself or selling your soul.

While you're trying to flatter and cajole your way into a problem supervisor's heart, try to deliver your "I really enjoy my job" speech to someone in the personnel department. They'll be uncomfortable speaking with you if they suspect you're intentionally bypassing your supervisor, so you must use some misdirection. Approach them with a question about your continuing-education program. Explain you've a choice of taking courses in two different areas and wanted some advice—after all, they're the career experts. If they refer you back to your supervisor, apologize and concentrate on your bribery. At least you've planted the continuing-education seed with them. If they do sit down to talk with you, use the education issue as a way to lead into your whole spiel.

Renewing your employment vows isn't the most enjoyable or exciting activity in the world. It's hard work and may require swallowing a little bit of your pride and giving up some of your individuality. But in exchange you'll receive something of immeasurable value in a recession—assurance of a solid stream of income. That's worth eating a little humble pie.

Ten Steps for Renewing Your Job Vows

1. Make sure you're well groomed and dressed according to the standards of your immediate supervisor.
2. Maintain and project a positive, can-do attitude. Smile and be friendly to underlings, peers, and superiors alike. Don't participate in gossip or character assassinations.
3. Arrive at work at least thirty minutes earlier and leave at least thirty minutes later than the officially stated hours.
4. Become a student of your company and industry and demonstrate your knowledge to others.
5. Find out what your company's goal is and then demonstrate how you're contributing to reaching it.
6. Show your interest and enthusiasm by offering suggestions on how things can be done better, quicker, or cheaper.
7. Establish and solidify your own power base.
8. Broaden your responsibilities and look for vacuums you can fill, without asking for additional compensation.
9. Add to your repertoire of skills and abilities through company training programs or continuing education—and let your superiors know about it.
10. Develop a positive personal relationship with your immediate superior.

CHAPTER 3

Making Your Business Lean and Mean

Humans must breathe,
but corporations must make money.
—Alice Embree

While employees are busy renewing their job vows, those who are self-employed similarly need to put their businesses through a cleansing acid bath to strip off the barnacles that have collected over the past ten years, and then take an objective look at their operation.

In the first few years of the business's life you were at your desk or behind the counter two hours early. You were the janitor as well as the chief executive officer. The business consumed your every waking moment—and your dreams as well. But during the 1980s things changed. In the past decade it was tough *not* to make it as an entrepreneur. Consumers were buying everything in sight, often for inflated prices; and bankers were actually soliciting borrowers. For a while it seemed all you had to do was scrape together some seed money, open a store selling designer popcorn, and suddenly customers were banging down the doors and bankers were calling on the telephone. Before you knew it, you were arriving at the business just before it opened and leaving at closing time. You hired an assistant—and then he hired an assistant as well. Rather than pouring the money back into operations you started renovating your home and vacationing in St. Bart.

But now things have changed. Customers have stopped banging on your doors. In fact, except for a few regulars, the stream of enthusiastic buyers has all but dried up. The banker who three years ago was prodding you to borrow money telephoned last week "just to see how things are going," to remind you your seasonal line of credit must be cleaned up by the end of next month, and to hint it may not be renewed.

You've thrown away the brochures on European vacations and have begun talking up to your family the idea of a weekend in the local mountains. And rather than buy the Miata you've been admiring for the past six months, you've decided to fix the transmission on the Subaru. In short you're nervous. Those life-style changes you've been contemplating are sound ideas, as you'll read in later chapters, but your first priority must be to check and reinforce your stream of income. And since you're an entrepreneur, that means streamlining your business.

In order to analyze and make informed decisions about what must be done, you need to have up-to-date financial data on the health and status of your business operations. If you don't have them at your fingertips, get them. Too many entrepreneurs run their businesses by the seat of the pants. They "have a feeling" for what they're spending, what they're bringing in, and how they're doing. Incredibly they're often right. But a recession is no time to rely on instinct and hunches. Without an accurate profile of your company's finances the only financial move you can make with impunity is to stop drawing a salary. Call your accountant and tell her you need a current profit-and-loss statement and balance sheet and you need it as soon as possible—even if you must pay double for the work because it's tax season. And make sure the accountant has accurate numbers, including an inventory count, to work with—this is not the time for creative bookkeeping.

While your accountant is pulling together the numbers, dig out your old business plan. Forget about the financial projections for a moment and concentrate on how you once described the business. Is it the business you're in today? Have you lost focus on your reason for being? Have you shifted emphasis away from core operations and out to the fringe? Sometimes it's hard to see the forest when you're stuck amid all the trees, and it's possible you've gotten caught up in running the day-to-day business process without realizing priorities were shifting. Take a look at how you described your target customer. Is it the person you're selling to today? Perhaps you've broadened your aim or shifted your target without even realizing it. Make sure that any shifts in your course were and are valid.

When your accountant finishes compiling the numbers, sit down with her for a heart-to-heart talk. Before you start working like a fiend to solidify your business, you need to know the effort is worthwhile. Many businesses that survived the 1980s did so only because the overall economic waters were pleasant. Now the economic seas are rough, and maybe it has become clear your business isn't seaworthy. Recessions are very good at uncovering hitherto unseen problems. If your accountant is unwilling or unable to help you make an honest judgment, find someone who is or who can. There's nothing wrong with selling or liquidating a business that is no longer viable. Entrepreneurs tend to start, run, and dissolve any number of businesses in their careers. Some of these operations have long life spans, and others don't. Some can be adapted to changing economic circumstances, and others can't. Maybe your business has simply become a habit. Perhaps it, and you, have been "just hanging on" for some time now without your realizing it. Don't mistake the simple absence of sufficient capital for lack of viability, however. (For information on how to acquire more capital, see chapter 15.)

But if you and your financial advisors are confident your operation is still viable, then roll up your sleeves for some hard work. You're going to take an inspection tour of the entire business, using the balance sheet and profit-and-loss statement as your map. While on this tour, you'll be looking for ways to streamline operations, increase revenue, and decrease expenses. The goal of this exercise is to maximize your business's stream of income, not only to ensure its current health but to free up funds which can then be used to take advantage of the unprecedented opportunities a recession offers—opportunities we'll examine in chapter 15.

The first leg of your tour is a visit to the balance sheet, and the first stop is the asset section. For most businesses the asset portion of the balance sheet consists of cash, accounts receivable, inventory, and plants and equipment. Let's start with cash.

For a business to maintain the best cash position, it has to do a delicate balancing act. Having too little means living from hand to mouth and being constantly under the threat of being wiped out by a short-term crisis, such as a regular customer not paying his bill on time or a flood destroying a portion of your inventory. Unless you've a cash cushion, your business may be injured by even a brief interruption in cash flow. However, having excess cash means you might not be taking advantage of all your opportunities. The return on money invested in your business will, or at least should, be three times greater than any interest you earn from a bank.

While the specific amount of cash needed varies from business to business—and can only be determined by you and your accountant—every entrepreneur's goal should be to have just enough and to get its maximum yield. If you don't have enough, start setting some aside. If you've too much, turn to chapter 15 and perhaps plan an expansion program. At least make sure it's invested in financial instruments that give you the best return. Read the advice on investing a personal cash reserve found in chapter 13, and apply the same rules to your business's cash. Consider the short-term cash investments and tools offered by your bank as well. Many commercial banks offer account-sweeping programs, in which a business's funds are invested in short-term commercial paper either overnight or over a weekend and are then returned with interest.

After analyzing your cash position, turn next to accounts receivable. When times are good, it's easy to get lax about collecting your money speedily. You want customers to think you're nice, so you don't put too much pressure on slow payers. So much of your energy is devoted to keeping up with orders or projects, there's little time left to follow up on your billing and collections. In a recession this has to stop. If business is slow, you now have the time; and if it's not, you've got to make the time. Begin by categorizing all your accounts receivable by date (i.e., thirty, sixty, ninety days). Calculate which accounts are past due, for how long, and how much is owed.

While it's nearly impossible to have completely current receivables, they should at least match your industry's standard. By extending credit you're in effect serving as a banker for your customers. And as you'll read in the next chapter, that's not a good business to be in during a recession. In order to trim your overdue accounts receivable and get out of the banking business, you must make some delicate telephone calls or visits to regular customers.

Business is tough for everyone these days, and some of your longtime clients are probably slowing down their payments—as you'll soon be doing if you aren't already—in order to get the most benefit from their money. You don't want to alienate good customers, but you do want to get your money as soon as possible. The answer is to blame the situation on someone else. Call slow-paying customers and explain that while in the past they've been taking sixty days to pay, the bank is on your back to speed up collections. Politely ask if they can pay their outstanding balance and say that in the future you'd love for them to pay invoices within thirty days.

If they have a problem coming up with the cash right now, offer to take a promissory note for the portion of the bill that is more than 30 days past due. Explain this would allow you to take the numbers out of "accounts receivable" and put it in another section of the balance sheet—"notes receivable"—thus making your banker happy. Actually this maneuver is as much for your benefit.

Asking for a note may be enough of a prod to get the cash out of a customer who's just being tightfisted. In addition it's easy and more affordable to borrow against a note than against accounts receivable. And if the customer *is* having financial problems, you're better off with a note than an unpaid invoice. If a claim goes to litigation, proving they purchased something and didn't pay for it can take a long time. Having a note allows you to file for a summary judgment instead of having to prove the claim, enabling you to collect the money much faster.

While reeling in current customers' receivables, you must also keep a tight rein on new customers. Even though new business may be tough to come by right now, it's important to realize that lots of people and businesses are struggling. Some of these new people may be coming to you because they couldn't get credit elsewhere. Redouble your credit-checking efforts and ask for deposits from new customers. Be gracious but firm. Say that while you want their business, you need to have some money up front. Ask for an amount equivalent to your cost and overhead. If this presents a problem, offer to accept a letter of credit from their bank instead. This serves as your guarantee of payment. If they still have a problem, consider declining the business. You can't afford to go too far out on a limb during this recession—especially with customers you've never dealt with before.

With your new credit policies in place, investigate adding cash-management services to your arsenal of business tools. Consider adding a lockbox service if your bank offers it. A lockbox is an account at a distant location that lets you use monies deposited there as if they where from local sources. Let me explain. If you're located in Los Angeles but have customers in New York and Philadelphia, it probably takes at least seven days for their checks to clear and for you to be able to use their funds. This period is called the float. It represents seven days of lost interest. By opening a lockbox account, in this case, in New Jersey, you can get immediate access to those New York and Philadelphia checks and eliminate the float.

With your accounts receivables minimized, move to the next item on the asset list: inventory. When was the last time you actually physically checked your inventory? Unless your accountant certifies your inventory at the end of each fiscal year, I'll bet it's been years since you've personally examined every item gathering dust in your storeroom, basement, or warehouse. You've come to rely on paper, or even electronic data, rather than gathering information with your eyes. This, too, has to stop. Before you can take measures to streamline your inventory, you must physically examine it—even if it takes a few days and you must pay your staff overtime to help out.

Chances are you've more inventory than you need. It's tough to keep inventory tight, especially when business is good. You see a chance to buy in bulk and save money. You're afraid of running out of an item, so you overbuy, just in case. From now on, however, you're going to shift from a "just in case" to a "just in time" inventory philosophy. The more often your inventory turns over, the healthier your business. Suppliers are well aware of this need, and increasing numbers of them are willing to work with you. Some are even setting up direct links between your business and their factory, which can result in next-day deliveries.

But even as you're changing inventory philosophies, you need to do something about all the stuff piled up downstairs. Divide your stock into salable and nonsalable goods. The latter would include obsolete, dirty, and broken goods. If you've too many items of any one particular type of salable goods, add the excess items to the nonsalable category. Your goal is to get nonsalable inventory to somehow help your cash flow.

Try to return unsold goods to suppliers. It's unlikely you can get them to refund your money, so try instead to have broken items refurbished or reconditioned. If packages are damaged or dirty, ask for the goods inside to be repackaged. Take outdated or excessive merchandise and try to sell it quickly through dramatic discounts or bulk-buying plans. For example, shrink-wrap four items together and sell it for the price of three ... or two. If all your efforts at selling stale items fail, donate it to charities. At least you'll get a write-off for it.

One of the brightest entrepreneurs I ever met was president of a small vitamin company located in a suburb of New York City. His business was subject to spurts of fad buying whenever a new medical study indicating the benefits of one vitamin or another was published. When the fad died down, or was replaced by another, he often found himself overstocked. Rather than let the excess merchandise sit and gather dust, as soon as he sensed the demand was wavering, he'd shrink-wrap three bottles together and sell them for the price of two. He still made a profit and more importantly he kept his inventory trim.

The final item on the asset side of your balance sheet is plants and equipment. While combined on the financial statement, plants and equipment need to be examined separately.

If the economic boom or tax advantages led you to open multiple facilities in the past decade, now is the time to reexamine the decision. Just because you own a plant doesn't mean you must operate a business in it. Perhaps you opened a remote facility and moved one part of your operation there in order to take advantage of the incentives the state offered to businesses. Tax breaks and cheap loans are no longer good enough reasons to maintain money-losing facilities. Judge each of your locations on their individual financial merits, and if consolidation is called for, do it. Unused plants can be sold or turned into rental property instead. And even if they're forced to remain vacant for a period of time, it's better than throwing more money down the drain.

One client of mine went overboard opening up facilities in the early 1980s. At that time some states with high unemployment rates were offering very attractive terms, including low-interest loans and free employee training, to manufacturers that opened plants in depressed communities. All the added benefits and tax write-offs seduced him into overexpanding. Luckily he spotted the recession coming and has been in the process of closing down his unprofitable facilities. His name may be mud in the towns where he has shut plants, but his business is weathering the recession and his remaining employees are secure.

All the easy money of the 1980s may have led you to buy lots of equipment for your business. But now with money tight, buying no longer makes much sense. If the equipment you currently own is still good, maintain it. If it's obsolete, sell it and lease new equipment instead. Leasing offers risk-free use of assets without a sizable investment—the perfect combination in a recession. Sell your obsolete computers and copying machines, and aging cars and trucks, and lease replacements.

The next stop on this first leg of your inspection tour is the liabilities side of the balance sheet, which consists primarily of accounts payable and bank debt. Let's examine your accounts payable first.

Your instinctive response may be to slow down payment of your bills. But that's not always the wisest choice. When working with suppliers that permit discounts, it may make more sense to pay sooner rather than later. If a regular supplier offers you a 2 percent discount on bills paid within ten days, take advantage of it. Over the course of a year this amounts to a 24 percent yield on your funds—more than you'll get anywhere else. However, your payments to suppliers that don't offer discounts should be slowed down as much as possible.

The secret to slowing payment is not to surprise the other party. Schedule a meeting with your nondiscount suppliers and explain your situation. Again, blame it on your banker if you must. Say that while in the past you've always paid on time, for the next few months you need to stretch payment out another fifteen or thirty days, to clean up your financial ratios and please your picky banker. Eager to keep customers, and grateful you've given them a warning, most suppliers will grudgingly grin and bear it as a cost of doing business during the recession.

One further step you may want to take to streamline your accounts payable is to open a checking account on the other side of the country. Just as a lockbox account speeds up collection of accounts receivable, a remote checking account slows down accounts payable. This will let you take advantage of the float, once again adding as much as seven days' interest to your coffers.

The final, and probably largest, item on the liabilities side of the balance sheet is bank debt. Throughout the 1980s your banker was probably encouraging you to borrow funds for expansion, growth, operating capital, a new car, new computers—anything you wanted. And to be honest, the banker probably didn't need to twist your arm too hard. When lenders, who are supposed to be careful with their money, urge you to borrow, worries over whether it's actually wise quickly fly out the window. If you're like most business people, during the 1980s you borrowed as much as you could, not as much as you should. But now it's the 1990s and the recession has tightened spending and lending, turning each of those bank loans into a sword of Damocles

precariously suspended over your head by a single
hair. It's essential to take preemptive action right
away, before it decapitates your business, to reduce
your monthly debt payments.

Contact your banker immediately, and set up an
appointment to meet with him. Meanwhile telephone
your accountant again and tell her you've another rush
job. Not only must your banker present loan-renegotia-
tion proposals to a committee, but he's also under the
watchful eye of a new breed of very sharp examiner.
The more thorough your financial data, the more
readily they'll all agree to your request. Have the accountant prepare another set of financial statements,
this time budgeting the renegotiated loan you'll be asking for.

Rather than asking for the maturity of your loan
to be extended, push for lowered monthly payments in
return for paying a large balloon payment when the
loan matures. Your package should also include a cash-
flow statement projecting your monthly operational
budget for at least the term of the loan. And make sure
the statement indicates the loan has at least 125 to 150
percent coverage. For example, if your loan payments
total $12,000 per year, you should project a yearly cash
surplus of at least $6,000. This assures the bank the
loan terms work. Of course the more coverage you can
realistically project, the more likely they'll be to go
along with the loan.

While you're at it, read chapter 15 and try to project any future loans you may need for expansion or ac-
quisitions. It's easier to come to the banker with a
single package combining renegotiation and additional
funds than to come back a second time for more
money.

When you present your proposal to the banker,
stress that you're doing this to "reposition" the busi-

ness because "opportunities for growth are being limited," not because you're in trouble. Be direct with the banker, explaining how much you need, why, and what you'll use it for. This demonstrates business acumen as well as honesty. Banks are always reticent about foreclosing on loans—it's not good for business. And a recent spate of successful lender-liability lawsuits have made them even more willing to renegotiate, so your chances for approval are good. If you're offered less than is needed, don't accept it. Ask the banker for time to find another, more generous lender. You can always come back and accept this offer if there are no other options, and the threat of taking your business elsewhere may prod the first banker into a concession.

The first leg of your inspection tour is over. The second and final portion is a thorough analysis of the business's profit-and-loss statement—more specifically, an examination of all your expenses.

When a business is being launched, entrepreneurs investigate, compare, and negotiate every single item in their budget. Nothing is too small to haggle over. But once a business is up and running, expenses have a way of insidiously growing. The savvy, comparison-shopping entrepreneur, busy doing a million and one other things, stops focusing on individual expenses. Prices and fees increase, and unless the jumps are sizable, they're simply added to, or rather subtracted from, the bottom line. Signing checks becomes a mindless task rather than a reasoned process for most busy owner/operators. This lack of attention has to stop. Tell your bookkeeper that the next time bills are going to be paid, you want to draw the checks as well as sign them. I guarantee you'll be shocked.

I know I was when I wrote out the checks for my business one month earlier this year. I knew my payroll had grown, but I couldn't believe how much more

I was spending on employee medical insurance. Even smaller expenses, such as magazine subscriptions, had grown geometrically. I came away from the experience angry and frustrated. But rather than rail against the evils of inflation, as I did, use your anger as a motivating device. Vow that from now on you'll keep at least one eye glued to your expenses. Meanwhile, start looking for places to cut.

Your largest single expense item is probably labor. Run a finger down your payroll and calculate the number of employees who have assistants. Then figure out how many of the assistants have assistants. The point I'm trying to make is that payroll often grows ahead of need. In many cases positions are added to your company because someone wants to hand over a part of his job he doesn't like. For example, your office manager may hate updating the ledgers, so he builds a case for hiring a full-time bookkeeper. Entrepreneurs are as guilty of this as any employee. In the early days you did whatever was needed, whether it meant doing the books, cleaning the bathroom, or typing letters. But as the business grew, you passed the less important and less interesting jobs on to others. In this recession, however, you and your managers must add some of those annoying tasks back to your job descriptions.

I believe that almost every business can afford to lay off at least one person—if the entrepreneur is willing to take that person's place. I don't mean you must physically do the same job. But by taking on more work yourself—becoming a worker, not just a thinker—and distributing the laid-off employee's responsibilities among the rest of the staff, you can pick up the slack. Use this as an opportunity to rid yourself of a troublemaker if you have one. (Watch out for potential claims for wrongful termination.) If not, let the least well-rounded person go. Since work is to be redistributed and job definitions changed, flexibility in staffers is a priority.

Your task, as heinous as it may be, is to select a recession sacrifice. I know it's not easy to let someone go. Even when the person being laid off isn't a good worker, the guilt feelings are powerful. You're firing not just the employee, but his family too. You feel as if you're condemning someone to death and then executing them. The only solace I can offer is the following: Don't look at this as something you're doing for your benefit alone. It's for your family as well. And it's for the benefit of all your other employees and their families as well. Unless the business makes it through this recession, you, your family, your staff, and their families, will all suffer. You can also relieve some of the guilt by providing as sizable a severance package as the business can afford. Read chapter 7 for an idea of what the laid-off employee is feeling and trying to do. Don't rush to get rid of the condemned. Once you've selected someone, put the execution on the back burner until you complete planning the rest of your labor cost cutting.

Consider a freeze on all further hiring. While this is an excellent time to hire since the job market is crowded, you must make sure the business actually needs more people. Whenever a request is made to add a position, try to determine why another person is needed. If it's just because someone wants to trim an odious task from her job description, don't do it—even if that someone is you. If it's because volume has increased, consider hiring temporary help, a part-timer, or farming the job out to a free-lancer, before you actually hire another employee. The cost savings are substantial—perhaps as much as 20 percent, since you don't have to pay for benefits.

Calculate whether you can afford to give raises and

bonuses this year, and if so, how much. Don't worry about what you did last year. This is a recession and you can no longer make budgetary decisions based on the past. Similarly there's no law against foregoing holiday gifts in tough times, as long as there are no exceptions. Every budget item now starts at zero.

Once all your labor-cutting tactics are ready, schedule the firing for the soonest Friday afternoon. Have severance, vacation, and salary checks, and a letter of recommendation, all drawn up in advance. Call the person into your office and ask someone else—either a manager or a stenographer—to sit in as an observer. Be direct. Tell her she's being let go for strictly economic reasons. Thank her for past efforts and express regrets, but stress you'd like her to leave immediately. Hand her the checks and recommendation letter. If she has something to say, listen. Do not reconsider your actions or let her stick around to use the facilities while looking for another job: her presence is terrible for morale. Instead, respond to all valid points with an increase in severance.

Once it's done, bring everyone together for a staff meeting. Tell them about the firing and the reasons behind it. It's better for the news to come from you than for it to filter down the grapevine. This lets you put the best possible spin on the situation. Announce your intention to take a more active role in day-to-day operations—in effect, to pick up the slack yourself. Stress that while the decision was difficult, you felt it was in everyone's best interests. Go on to describe the new insurance, hiring, bonus, and gift policies. This helps place the firing in perspective as but one part of an overall cost-cutting strategy. Reiterate that there are no exceptions, and demonstrate it by applying the new rules to yourself as well as to others. Without sounding condescending, explain that your goal is to save jobs by cutting costs. Conclude by thanking them all for their past labors and for future efforts. Remind them that the recession is only temporary and that things will turn around soon. State that if the company can tighten its belt now, it will be in a better position to take advantage of the coming economic resurgence.

With the hardest part behind you, move on to the next largest expense item: rent. Commercial real estate is truly in an economic free-fall. Prices are plummeting, and there's still no bottom in sight. Commercial landlords everywhere are feeling the pinch. That's what makes it a perfect time to get rent concessions—tenants have never had such leverage. The last thing your landlord needs is for one of his few paying tenants to leave. Approach the landlord and explain that your banker has been pressuring you to lower costs as a condition to renegotiating your term loan. Ask for a rent reduction for the next two years and offer in exchange to sign on for an additional five years at an increased rent. If you can't get a short-term rent reduction, try to get the landlord to assume the cost of improvements you'd like to make to the location.

Now turn to your insurance expenses. There's probably no other line on your profit-and-loss statement that has been increasing as rapidly, and this is the time to put a stop to it. Business coverage generally consists of two separate packages: property and casualty coverage and employee benefits. It's relatively easy to cut property and casualty costs. Simply ask five or six reputable brokers to bid on your coverage. There's up to a 20 percent swing in premiums today, and a broker who's hungry for business—as most are in this recession—will be able to put together a good cost-saving package. One retailer friend of mine was able to save $8,000 just by putting his current policies out for competitive bid.

Cutting your employee benefits insurance cost is more complicated, but it can be done. The secret to cutting the largest part of this coverage—health insurance—is to take a two-pronged approach of cost sharing and managed care. Cost sharing means taking a higher deductible and adding a co-insurance element to the plan so that employees pick up more of the cost of their own health care. Managed care refers to putting in place certain requirements that can greatly reduce costs. Some examples are mandatory second opinions before surgery, preadmissions testing, and use of extended-care facilities or home-care services in lieu of prolonged hospital stays. Another element of managed care would be steering employees to lower-cost providers, either through health maintenance organizations and health insurance plans—in which they're limited to certain providers—or through preferred provider organizations, in which they're rewarded for using participating physicians.

Consider having regular health assessments—such as blood pressure and cholesterol checks—done at your site. Offer a one-time cash bonus to people who quit smoking for more than a month, with regular bonuses to follow for every month up to a year. Not only are such preventative measures effective in cutting premium costs, but they serve as morale boosters, demonstrating to employees that you really do care about their well-being.

You can cut other benefits insurance costs by turning the business's package into a smorgasbord. Rather than paying for the highest common denominator, you can use the diversity of the work force to your advantage. For example, not every employee needs health insurance. If an employee is covered under his spouse's health plan, he can select extended disability coverage from your smorgasbord. Perhaps you've younger employees with no dependents. Since they don't need life insurance, they may wish to take out a lower deductible on their health coverage. While the variations are endless, they all result in savings for you.

With insurance costs trimmed, focus on your marketing budget. Rather than cutting dollars here, look to redeploy resources where they'll have the most effect. Since the competition is probably cutting back on marketing, you can get a great deal more bang for your marketing buck during a recession. However, your efforts must be well targeted. Instead of spreading money across three radio stations and four newspapers in an effort to reach everyone, concentrate dollars where you know your customers are.

Do some informal market research. Try to obtain as much information about your customers as possible, either through warranty cards, informal questioning, or guest books. Then compare the profile of your customer with the profile of a radio station's listener, a magazine or newspaper's reader, or a television program's viewer. Spend the lion's share of your marketing dollars wherever you find the closest match.

Meanwhile don't overlook cooperative programs, which can help stretch your advertising budget even further. And redouble your public relations efforts. In many businesses publicity is both cheaper and more effective than advertising.

While labor, rent, insurance, and marketing are probably the four largest expense items on your profit-and-loss statement, they shouldn't be the only costs you cut. No expense is too small to be reexamined. Call in your professionals and ask them to lower their retainers or to bill you on an hourly basis with a budget. Trim back the business's holiday gift list and lower your per-gift budget. Eliminate memberships in professional clubs and associations that only provide ego benefits. Ask the local utility to conduct an energy audit of your facilities and implement their suggestions. Hold staff parties at lunch and in the office itself, rather than in restaurants after work. In my case I cut back on the use of overnight deliveries, faxing, and magazine subscriptions. Only items that absolutely, positively, must be there overnight are sent that way. We've gone back to using the mail rather than faxing almost everything. And instead of getting multiple subscriptions of publications, my office manager is now buying one copy at the newsstand and circulating it among all of us.

The hardest part of this entire process isn't making the cuts, it's keeping spirits up afterward. It's essential for you to wear a smile and project a positive attitude right now, otherwise these budgeting efforts come across as desperate measures. Clients and customers pick up on bad vibes and can turn worries into self-fulfilling prophecies. Keep things bullish and urge your employees to do the same. Foster a team spirit and an "us against the world" mentality. Let your employees know that you're in the same boat as they are and that when the recession is over, you'll make up for their sacrifices. You'll find your own spirits picking up as soon as you see the savings that result from your actions. Each dollar saved is like a little victory in the battle against the recession.

CHAPTER 4

Checking Your Financial Foundations

'Tis the part of a wise man to keep himself today for tomorrow,
and not venture all his eggs in one basket.
—Miguel de Cervantes

We all accept, at least subconsciously, that in exchange for the unparalleled opportunities it offers, the capitalist system also has risks: There are economic ups and downs; times when we do well and times when we don't; years when a dollar goes far and years when it doesn't. "Sure, it's a tragedy when a company lays off workers," we say, "but while one company is hurting and letting people go, another is thriving and creating new jobs." But our confidence was shattered when cracks began appearing in what we perceived to be the foundations of our economy, making this recession more mysterious and frightening than any other recent economic downturn.

Along with reports of layoffs and unemployment, the pages of our daily newspapers are filled with stories about banks failing, insurance companies teetering on the brink of bankruptcy, and struggling companies that are borrowing against employees' pension funds.

We can accept businesses going broke. We can understand municipalities going through a budget crisis—especially when we're going through one of our own. We
can even deal with savings and loan institutions going
belly-up, since our perception of them—erroneous as
it may have been—was as little mom-and-pop lenders
inexorably linked to local economies. But when leading
banks and major insurance companies start showing
signs of trouble and employers start gambling with retirement funds, we get nervous. Those lobbies of marble and massive vaults, and those Rocks of Gibraltar
and omnipresent umbrellas, were supposed to be removed from the vagaries of the market. How could
they possibly lose money? And how could a business
mortgage its employees' future? The answer to both
questions is simple: greed.

Like clockwork, every ten years a whole new gen-
eration of bankers appears on the scene. Since there's
no institutional memory in the banking business, these
newcomers invariably make the same mistake their
predecessors did a decade before: They forget that
banks are the tortoises of the financial world. Eager to
make names for themselves and add to the institution's
coffers, these young hotshots look to turn quick profits.
They forget that bankers must be discrete lenders since
they use depositors' money, not their own. And depositors only continue to put money in banks if they're sure
it will be safe. In their hunger for short-term profits,
the young bankers always begin to take greater risks.
They stop blending their investments and instead pursue a few big deals in an effort to cut down their per-
loan cost.

I know all about how young bankers think because
twenty years ago I was one myself. My specialty was
real estate, and I was always on the prowl, developing
deals that would make me look good. Rather than

write twenty one-million-dollar loans, I looked for the twenty-million-dollar deal, since it required less over-head and was therefore more cost-effective.

In the past this propensity for excessive risk taking was held in check by government regulation. When I was a young banker, I could only go so far. But, in accord with their economic philosophy, the Reaganauts removed many of the regulatory chains that shackled bankers. The advocates of deregulation didn't understand that it's fine to give institutions and companies freedom with their own money but it's wrong to give them too much freedom with other people's money.

Once unfettered, bankers leaped into leveraged buyouts: high-risk loans to parties wishing to stage hostile takeovers of other companies, loans that are backed by the perceived market value and potential profitability of the target company rather than by the borrower's actual assets. They began writing 80 and 90 percent mortgages and made business loans without regard to the quality of management. They jumped into commercial real estate—one of the riskiest of markets—with both feet. While gorging themselves on the up-front fees they made from investing their depositor's monies in these risky investments, they rationalized their bravado with reassurances that the FDIC was behind them and that the market would always go up. Their greed paid off handsomely, until the economy, stunted by consumer fears, began to slow.

Those high-interest leveraged buyout loans began to go sour. Now heavily burdened with debt, the value and health of many of these companies plummeted as quickly as they had previously risen. The residential and commercial real estate markets began to slow down and then shift into reverse. Bankers who loaned 80 to 90 percent of what they thought property was worth forgot that values are transitory. They found themselves in trouble when the actual value of the property dropped below even what they had loaned. Loans they made to marginal borrowers began to go into default. And since they had concentrated on a few big deals, rather than the spreading the risk over a great many smaller ones, each individual default had a mortal effect on the bank's financial health. When some banks tried to lend their way out of problems or make cosmetic corrections, they ran up against a new breed of bank examiner determined to hold them to the highest fiscal standards.

Being big was no defense—in fact it may have contributed to the dilemma. Smaller, local banks, which stuck to the traditional lending rules, didn't grow dramatically in the 1980s but are today as healthy as ever. Big banks, on the other hand, made big mistakes. Not only did they err on a larger scale but they also got involved in the international arena, making gigantic loans to countries that will never be able to pay them off. Even the federal government entered into the act by encouraging banks to continually recast their loans with friendly debtor nations rather than stop lending.

Size was no help to insurance companies either. Rather than concentrate on their core business—the underwriting of policies—some insurance company executives got caught up in the investment fervor of the 1980s. They lowered their underwriting standards and requirements in order to bring more premium dollars into the insurance company. The rationale was that the company could afford to lose money on underwriting so long as the added dollars brought in through the lowered standards could be invested at a sizable profit. Insurance companies began to view themselves as diversified investment organizations. Products, such as variable and universal life—in which the equity of policies was invested in the stock and bond markets—were developed to let policyholders join in this new insurance game.

Competitive pressures led to even riskier investments. High-yield/high-risk junk bonds began to appear in the portfolios of major insurance companies. Aggressive real estate lending became acceptable. And to make matters worse, some insurance companies took equity positions in these deals. If a bank's real estate loan went bad, at least it had only loaned a percentage of the property's value. Insurance companies with an equity position, on the other hand, matched the entrepreneur/developer dollar for dollar. The net result of all this wheeling and dealing is that some major insurance companies appear on the verge of bankruptcy and are on the "watch list" of many state insurance regulators.

Perhaps the easiest to understand, but maybe the most disgraceful crack in the foundation, is the use of pension funds as collateral for loans. It's a more common technique than you might think—even governments are using it to make up budget gaps. But despite its increased use it indicates a desperate need to raise cash, the lack of other unleveraged assets, and a shameful insensitivity to the safety of employees' money. None of which is good news for the employee. One variation on this technique that's also being used is the investment of pension funds in company stock. That's great if the company is dependable and growing, but extremely dangerous if it's not.

If all this talk of bank problems, insurance-company bankruptcies, and pension-plan chicanery instills a little fear in you, that's healthy. Such financial debacles can have serious impact on personal finances. However, it's not a sign the foundations of the economy are crumbling. Banking and insurance are not dead, nor even dying. In banking, for example, almost all the nearly 10,000 community banks with assets of less $100 million are fine. So are the nearly 2,500 mid-size regional banks with assets of less than $1 billion. Generally it's the larger banks—the ones who forgot the fundamentals—that are in trouble. Ten of the 48 banks that have assets of more than $10 billion lost money last year. There will be additional bank failures, probably as many if not more than last year, when 200 institutions shut down. But banks are far too well capitalized for them to suffer an overall disaster à la the savings and loan industry. Instead we will probably see widespread consolidations and mergers, resulting in fewer but more profitable institutions. Don't let the positive long-term outlook, however, deter you from investigating possible short-term problems.

The FDIC isn't a panacea for banking problems. It's a marvelous device for avoiding the wholesale bank rushes and subsequent failures we experienced in the Great Depression. When a bank appears in danger of failing, it's seized by the government, which assumes control of the institution and runs it until a buyer is found. The entire seizure process takes only a few hours and the inconvenience to customers is generally slight. If no buyer is found for the failed bank, the FDIC dissolves all the accounts and pays out up to $100,000 per depositor, including interest up to the date the account is closed.

But there are limits to what the FDIC actually promises to do for depositors. Its chartering regulations don't stipulate *when* depositors actually receive their money. When bank seizures are few and far between, depositors have almost immediate access. As increased numbers of banks are seized, however, the FDIC's meager reserves get stretched even thinner. In response it may restrict access for a period of time. If your bank is seized, you may not be able to get at your money for one, two, maybe even five days.

Interest rates aren't insured by the FDIC, either, and may be changed when business resumes. Certificates of deposit, which were locked in at a high-interest rate—let's say 10 percent—may shift to a passbook rate of 5 percent. Depositors will be informed of the change and given a chance to withdraw funds without a penalty, but that doesn't mean they'll be able to match what they were previously getting.

The same holds true for credit card interest. Many bankers today see increased interest rates on credit cards as their salvation since it's a low-risk/high-profit business. All a bank needs do is notify cardholders of a new rate. Dramatic increases can be slipped through without any fanfare.

Unused lines of credit aren't guaranteed by the FDIC, either, nor must be continued by subsequent owners of the bank. It's actually standard practice for all unused lines of credit—whether commercial or private—to be canceled as soon as a bank is taken over. Homeowners counting on paying their child's college tuition with a home-equity line of credit and businesses relying on seasonal borrowing to get through slow periods must reestablish their credit. That could be inconvenient, troublesome, perhaps even impossible in today's economic environment.

Changes in bank ownership can also spell trouble for homeowners with some types of adjustable-rate mortgages. Many of these mortgages have thirty-year terms, but mature every one to five years, allowing the interest rate to be adjusted. The mortgagee theoretically must reapply and be approved each time the loan matures. In the past this was little more than a formality. Banks simply rubber-stamped the application and raised the interest rate. When a bank has been seized or taken over, however, the new lender may have a different banking philosophy. Rather than making the re-application process a formality, it may use it as an opportunity to get out of loans not in keeping with the new philosophy. This is becoming increasingly common with second- or summer-home mortgages.

In truly perilous times bankers can use a fine-print clause present in almost all their loan agreements to call loans early. The standard "at risk" clause states that any time a bank feels it's in extreme jeopardy, it has the right to call the loan. This clause is rarely used, and I don't see it becoming a popular banking tool—it could completely destroy consumer trust in banking institutions. However, it's something you should be aware of. While there's nothing you can do about loans you've already signed, you can try to remove the clause in future loan negotiations.

Read any mail from your bank carefully, especially if you're in the habit of simply letting the institution roll your CDs over when they come due. A few Americans were badly burned this past year when troubled banks, rather than automatically rolling CDs over or placing the funds in a passbook savings account, decided to invest the money in their own commercial paper—which isn't insured by the FDIC. The banks duly notified depositors of the maneuver, but some paid no attention to it. When the banks went under, those who had ignored the notices found that their money was lost since it was uninsured.

Most people are less nervous about insurer failures than bank seizures, since they perceive insurance as a product rather than part of their financial portfolio. But they should be nervous, since insurance is actually an investment. Premiums paid to an insurer bear fruit when benefits are paid. And while the premiums are substantial, so are the potential benefits. Insurance can repair or replace your most expensive assets—your home and your car—as well as any other possessions that are damaged or destroyed. It can also pay for your medical care when ill and replace your income if you become disabled or die. Your retirement may also rely on insurance companies and their products, such as annuities or the guaranteed-investment contracts that back some 401K plans.

The failure of your insurance company hits your financial foundation very hard: There's no federal guarantee covering your insurance investments, and without coverage you've no safety net. Emergencies that occur must be paid for in cash. While younger individuals and businesses are able to turn around and purchase new liability and health policies if their current insurer goes bankrupt, it's much more difficult and expensive for older Americans to replace life and disability coverage.

I'm an unfortunate example of this problem. Thirty-five years ago I bought an extensive disability policy with a then-substantial insurance company. I recently discovered this once-solid insurer is now in very poor financial shape and may declare bankruptcy in the coming year. I did some investigating and discovered that purchasing the same coverage today will cost three times what I'm currently paying.

The first step in dealing with the potential instability of banks, insurance companies, and pension plans is to enlist the aid of a professional. While it's possible to do some of the research yourself, much of what you need is buried deep within financial statements that the institutions try to keep from prying eyes and is covered with layers of legalese. By the time you're able to uncover and analyze all the data, your bank or insurance company may have already gone bankrupt. Instead, seek out a certified financial planner who charges an hourly fee for his or her services rather than a commission.

Disregard any calls from salespeople or insurance agents urging you to shift your funds or coverage to them and away from your current bank or insurer. It's in their best interest for you to rearrange your finances. Accept their words of warning, but don't act on them until they're verified by an unbiased expert.

Ask your attorney or accountant to recommend a financial planner. Don't spend too much time on the selection of the planner for this job. You aren't looking for advice just yet, just financial research, so almost any competent professional will do. You can get choosy later on in chapter 13, when we discuss your investment life. Tell the person that while in the coming weeks you'll be looking for someone to provide a complete consultation, your immediate concern is the health of your bank, insurers, and pension plan. Rather than an opinion, you're looking for information. You want to know if there are any warning signs. For a list of the various warning signs of possible bank, insurance company, and pension fund trouble, see the lists on pages 69 to 71.

Ask the planner how long it will take to come up with this information and how much he'll charge you for doing the research. It should take a skilled planner no longer than one to one and a half hours to come up with this information and should cost you no more than $75 to $150. It's money well spent whatever the outcome of the investigation. If you discover that part of your financial foundation is shaky, you've a chance to shore it up. If you find all's well, you'll be able to sleep well at night.

If the planner telephones you back with news that your bank is in serious trouble, take immediate action. Rather than heading down to your local branch—

where the lines may stretch around the block—go to another, safer financial institution and open new checking and money market accounts with checks drawn on your accounts at the troubled bank. Even if you fall well under the $100,000 limit, a takeover could freeze your money for a few days, and in a recession liquidity is vital. If you're above the $100,000 safety mark, break your accounts or CDs to get down to the limit of FDIC coverage, even if you must pay penalties. Remember, there's no guarantee the FDIC will make good on accounts over $100,000.

While the FDIC sometimes does insure all of a bank's accounts, regardless of size, the decision is made on a case-by-case basis. When the Freedom Bank in New York City failed in 1990, the FDIC stuck to its $100,000 limit, even though many of the bank's larger accounts belonged to not-for-profit organizations. On the other hand, when the Bank of New England failed in early 1991, the FDIC guaranteed all accounts regardless of their size. Why? Many of the larger Bank of New England depositors were businesses. Forcing them to absorb losses, the FDIC opined, could lead to a domino effect of regional bankruptcies.

How you react to the news that an insurer is in trouble depends on what they're insuring. If it's the company that carries your homeowner's, auto, health, or business insurance, you should immediately switch to another company. (For information on determining your insurance needs and soliciting bids for coverage during a recession, see chapter 5.) On the other hand, if it's your life or disability insurance company that's in trouble, you've got some thinking to do. Entirely shifting these policies to more-secure carriers guarantees that you won't need to deal with a bankrupt insurer. But it also guarantees that your premium bills will soar, since they were based on your age at the time of purchase. The best thing to do is hedge your bets. Cut your coverage with the carrier that's in danger in half and take out a new policy with a more secure company for the remainder. This assures you of continued coverage while minimizing the increase in your premium. If your original insurer does go bankrupt, you'll just be required to turn around and double the coverage in your second policy. That's what I've done with my disability insurance.

If you discover your pension plan isn't stable, find out if you can pull out of it, or borrow against it—even if there are penalties involved. Getting something is better than getting nothing. Unfortunately most pension plans are not portable and don't allow employees to use them as collateral. If you're involved in an employee stock ownership plan (ESOP), I'd give serious thought to selling out if possible. It's the ultimate in being undiversified—your investment life and job are both in the same place. Your employer going broke or falling on hard times is bad enough when it just affects your job; if it impacts on your investments as well, it's a catastrophe.

Let's say your company has a nonqualified pension plan in which it segregates your deferred compensation until you're eligible to receive it some time in the future. Initially you may have liked the setup, since you didn't pay taxes on the money. But since the funds legally belong to your employer until they're paid out, if the company declares bankruptcy, creditors can go after the money. You could end up with nothing. So whatever the condition of your employer-sponsored pension, it's time to stop relying on it alone to finance your retirement. That means establishing some type of independent retirement plan—whether it's taxable or not.

When the planner's information indicates your

bank, insurers, and pension plan are solvent, you've got time—ten minutes or so—to breathe a sigh of relief before you get to work. In a recession, savings, insurance, and retirement money should be spread among more than one bank, insurer, or pension plan. In the past we all tried to maximize leverage by concentrating business with one bank and insurance company. That made sense in good times, when these institutions were healthy and competing for business. We also used to rely on our company's pension as being both secure and sufficient to fund our retirement. In a recession, however, the potential benefits of concentrating your business with one institution, provider, or plan are outweighed by the danger of putting all your eggs in one, potentially flimsy basket.

While you're spreading your eggs among different baskets, don't forget to do the same with your stock portfolio if it's held by a brokerage firm. While the federally backed Securities Investor Protection Corporation insures your brokerage account up to $500,000, only $100,000 of that coverage applies to cash that may remain in your account after stocks are sold. Either make sure your account never has that much idle cash in it or spread your business among more than one firm. And don't be misled by advertising claims about insured mutual funds. Mutual funds are only actually protected to the extent that their individual holdings are backed by private insurers. Watch out for securities held in a "street name" rather than in your actual name. While this lets the brokerage house buy and sell with greater speed, there's a danger to the practice. If the brokerage firm goes into receivership or bankruptcy, it could take quite some time to sift through the paperwork and prove exactly who owns what.

It's ironic, but by using one of the very principles

that bankers and insurance executives forgot—spreading risks—you can protect yourself from their folly and make sure the foundations of your personal finances, savings, insurance, and retirement funds are safe and secure.

Warning Signs of Possible Bank Instability

- High turnover among officers
- Sloppy record keeping and paperwork
- Soliciting unnecessary credit extensions
- Unusually large increase in loan yield
- Loan recover rate below 20 percent
- Capital less than 6 percent of total assets
- Lower return on assets than similar institutions
- Overhead more than 56 percent of income base
- Downward trends in value of the bank's own stock
- Loan portfolio not sufficiently diversified
- Investment portfolio contains high-risk instruments
- Moody's and Standard & Poors ratings downgraded

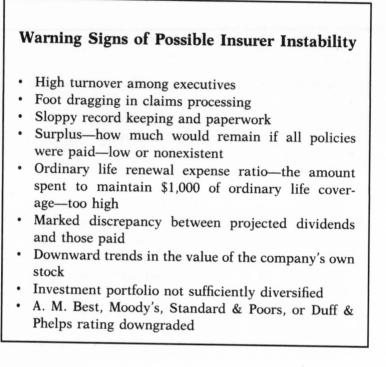

Warning Signs of Possible Insurer Instability

- High turnover among executives
- Foot dragging in claims processing
- Sloppy record keeping and paperwork
- Surplus—how much would remain if all policies were paid—low or nonexistent
- Ordinary life renewal expense ratio—the amount spent to maintain $1,000 of ordinary life coverage—too high
- Marked discrepancy between projected dividends and those paid
- Downward trends in the value of the company's own stock
- Investment portfolio not sufficiently diversified
- A. M. Best, Moody's, Standard & Poors, or Duff & Phelps rating downgraded

Warning Signs of Possible Pension Fund Instability

- Borrowed against by employer
- Tied up in stocks that are dwindling in value—including those of the company itself
- Assuming too high a rate of return
- Assumptions about employee turnover overstated
- Hasn't taken into account wage and salary increases
- Assets' market values lower than book values

CHAPTER 5

Trimming Debt and Establishing a Cash Reserve

Ah, take the Cash, and let the Credit go,
Nor heed the rumble of a distant Drum!
—Edward FitzGerald

Now that you've started "making love" to your boss and checked the health of your bank, insurance companies, and pension plan, the next step in solidifying your recession defenses is establishing a cash reserve equal to six months of your living expenses.

I can hear the laughter already. From the day you started working, people have been telling you to take a little bit from each paycheck and put it away for a rainy day. You've meant to do just that—but something always came up. Now I come along and tell you to set aside six months' worth of expenses, when you probably haven't even saved two weeks' salary.

Don't think you're the only one—almost everyone is in the same boat. We live from hand to mouth, regardless of our income. Bank accounts have turned into nothing more than pit stops for money. No matter how much we take home, it seems, we can't get ahead.

Raises are immediately swallowed up by rising costs and taxes, and if we're lucky, we break even in the process. If we do manage to squirrel away some money, it's inevitably eaten up by some unforeseen event—the car breaks down, the kids need braces, or the oil burner gives up the ghost.

But from the moment you read these words, things must change. Saving money is no longer a goal—it's a matter of survival. You need a six-month reserve during the recession to make it through an emergency. What happens if, heaven forbid, you lose your job? Renewing your employment vows may not have been enough, especially if the company was on the skids to begin with. Now you're out in a job market where positions are hard to come by. What if you don't have enough money in the bank to pay your rent, or your mortgage payment, or your insurance premiums? Without a six-month reserve you may be forced to take the first thing that comes along—whether or not it's right for you—just to pay your bills.

It's not only a question of your physical survival. In the event of a financial catastrophe—such as losing your job during a recession—an individual needs time to take stock of the situation, to think, and to plan. The instinctive responses in such situations are always the worst, since they're inspired by panic, not logic. Those who panic in tough times end up drowning. Those who keep their heads remain afloat and generally end up better off than they were before the catastrophe struck. In later chapters I'll tell you how, in a recession, to get the most from your company if you're fired, deal with financial emergencies, and speed up job searches. But for now let's concentrate on getting a six-month reserve started.

Obviously the secret of saving money is for your income to be greater than your expenses. If you're currently breaking even—the bills are getting paid, but there's no money left over at the end of the month—you can begin to build up a cash reserve in one of two ways: boosting income or trimming expenses. Again an obvious point. While there are ways to increase your income during a recession—some of which I describe in part III of this book—they all involve planning; none bear fruit right away. The establishment of a six-month cash reserve, however, is an immediate short-term goal. We can't wait for gambits to start paying off. We must begin now. That means concentrating on expenses.

There are two types of expenses: Those that are the same each month, and those that depend on your actions or circumstances. Businesses call these categories fixed and variable expenses. An individual's fixed expenses might include rent or mortgage payment, income and property taxes, insurance premiums, and debt service. Variable expenses include food, clothing, utilities, telephone, entertainment, and travel. Because we view fixed expenses as being etched in stone and variable expenses as being a product of behavior, we always focus on the latter when looking to trim spending.

From a long-term perspective it makes sense. By just slightly altering your life-style it's often possible to start saving money. But you cannot rely on behavioral changes—however motivated you are—to save you six months' worth of expenses quickly. Attitudes toward money and spending patterns are more deeply ingrained and habitual than almost any other traits. From a psychological point of view, they're formed in infancy and are as hard to kick as addictions. It can be done—later in this chapter I'll discuss how—but it's a difficult process that doesn't yield sizable immediate results. In order to start your emergency savings plan, you must first focus on trimming fixed expenses.

A very large portion of your fixed expenses—mortgage payments, car loan payments, credit card balances—are debt related. During the 1980s debt became respectable. A great many people, myself included I'm afraid, became enamored of the power of leverage. By borrowing money we could do and have today what we otherwise couldn't do or have until years later. Rather than saving up for a trip to France, we could borrow the money and go there now; we could get to see the Eiffel Tower while we were still young enough to climb the steps to the top. And to top it all off, the interest was tax deductible, so we could claim that borrowing made some financial sense: We could use future dollars, which would be worth less due to inflation, to pay today's bills. Consumers weren't alone in this regard. Businesses, bankers, insurance companies, and city and state governments all fell in love with debt for much the same reason. In fact debt became the fuel that ran the expanding economy of the 1980s.

But we all missed one essential point. We based leverage decisions on how much we *could* borrow rather than how much we *should* borrow. Instead of paying for essentials and then setting aside something for savings and/or investments, we kept borrowing until almost all our stream of income was tied up in paying off loans. We forgot that one day the bill would come due. And when the new tax regulations eliminated the deduction for consumer interest, the bill became a lot more painful. The inability to save money, I believe, is directly linked to excessive debt load. Freeing your stream of income from excessive debt allows you to begin saving money.

First, stop adding to your debt. Take all the credit cards out of your wallet and put them in a safe-deposit box. Keep one charge card handy for emergencies.

From now on you'll be paying cash or writing a check for almost all purchases. Credit cards anesthetize the buying process. When you pay cash or write a check, you actually see the dollars leave your hands. It helps bring the result of the transaction into sharp focus and gives you a moment to reflect on the wisdom of your actions. Charge cards that require you to pay in full when you get the bill, while theoretically short-term credit tools, are really just a convenience, helping you to minimize check writing and record keeping.

The only debts you should incur during a recession are those that are both necessary and large. By all means borrow to buy a new home, renovate your present home, send your child to college, or pay for medical care. No one has enough cash to pay for these, and, in the final analysis, they're more investments than expenses. Just stop borrowing to buy little things and luxury items.

After removing those tempting plastic cards from your wallet, figure out exactly how much you owe. Take out a piece of paper and divide it into four columns or use the work sheet on page 86. In the first column write down the name and type of the loan: home mortgage, car loan, MasterCard, Visa, and student loan, for example. Next, in the second column, write down the total balance of the loan—how much it would cost you to pay it off completely today. In the third column put down the interest rate that's being charged on the balance of the loan. For example: 12 percent for the mortgage, 10 percent for the car loan, 6 percent for the student loan, and 19 percent for the credit cards. In the last column write down the amount of your monthly payment. For your credit cards write down the minimum payment required on your last bill. In order to calculate exactly how much you owe, total the numbers in the second column. To see how much of your monthly fixed expenses are debt related, simply total up the numbers in the fourth column. To start saving, you must minimize one or both numbers.

One way to do that is regain the tax-deductible status lost when Congress changed the law. If you own a home and haven't yet investigated taking out an equity loan, now is the time to do so. Up to $100,000 of home equity debt is deductible. By using this money to pay off your other, nondeductible loans, you'll save a considerable amount of cash each month. Let me explain. Let's say you owe $10,000 on a 14 percent car loan and another $8,000 on a credit card that charges 19 percent. If you take out a home equity loan and pay off the car loan and credit cards, you'll still owe the $18,000, but you'll be paying only, perhaps, 11 percent interest. And this 11 percent, depending on your tax bracket, may actually only have the impact of 8 percent, since it's tax deductible.

In fact, taking out a home equity line of credit may be a good idea even if you don't have much non-tax-deductible debt to eliminate. While a low-interest, tax-deductible line of credit isn't a replacement for cash reserves, it's a good tool to have at your disposal during a recession. If you do opt to add this tool to your arsenal, just make sure the loan terms make sense and the lender is in solid shape.

During a recession it also may make sense to use your savings to pay off nondeductible debts if you can do it without damaging your liquidity or stream of income. The $10,000 deposited in a CD earning 6 or 7 percent interest can be more productive if it's used to pay off your 14 percent car loan. The $5,000 locked up in an 8 percent bond is more effectively used paying off your 19 percent credit card debt. You'll end up lowering your monthly expenses, and the savings can be earmarked for your cash reserves. Of course low-interest loans, such as government-sponsored education loans, should be left alone.

Finally, even though it's already tax deductible, take a close look at your mortgage. Interest rates on home loans are down right now, so refinancing your mortgage will probably result in lower monthly payments. How quickly you'll realize those savings, and how substantial they'll be, depends on your particular situation. While the standard rule of thumb has been to refinance if you can save two or more points of interest, you must do the calculations yourself. You can use the work sheet on page 86.

For example, let's say you've a thirty-year, adjustable-rate, $100,000, 11.5 percent mortgage on which you're paying $990 per month. If you refinance the entire mortgage and obtain a thirty-year, fixed-rate, 9.5 percent mortgage, your monthly payment drops to $841. That's a monthly saving of $149, and a yearly savings of $1,788—not bad at all. However, you must also figure in the costs you'll incur by refinancing. There are lots of low- and some no-point loans available today, so let's assume you'll be paying one point. One percent, or point, of $100,000 equals $1,000. In addition you must pay the bank's attorney and your own lawyer. That will probably cost you about $300 and $500 respectively. Finally you must pay an application and appraisal fee of around $200. Your total fees, therefore, will be $2,000. If you divide this total by your monthly savings, you'll find it takes you fourteen months to cover your costs and start pocketing the savings. Until then you'd actually be paying slightly more each month than if you hadn't refinanced.

Without knowing the specific circumstances of your life I can't tell you whether or not you should refinance your mortgage—there are no general rules. I *can* tell you that, in my opinion, mortgage rates are not going to drop much farther. If you've a chance to lock in for thirty years at a fixed rate of less than 10 percent, I advise you to do it. The tremendous long-term savings far outweigh the slight short-term added cost. Think about it: Using the example illustrated above, you'd save about $51,500 over the thirty-year term of the mortgage in exchange for paying around $17 more for fourteen months.

Eliminating and streamlining your debts alone won't provide you with a six-month cash reserve. But by minimizing the amount of money spent each month on debt service, and by turning as much of it as is possible into a tax-deductible expense, you'll probably be able to save between two and three months' worth of expenses over the course of a year. While that's a good start—it's not enough.

The next place to look to minimize your spending are insurance premiums. Most Americans are very lazy insurance consumers, perhaps because it's a negative, almost depressing, purchase. Discussion of possible death, illness, disability, and disaster aren't anyone's idea of a good time—so it's avoided whenever possible. Few people actually shop around for the best coverage, choosing instead to rely on an agent who was referred by a friend or relative. And almost no one changes carriers once they've signed up—even though there are price differences of up to 20 percent on the same coverage from insurer to insurer.

Now that we're struggling to scrape together six months' cash reserve to weather the recession, complacency and avoiding unpleasant topics are two luxuries we can no longer afford. It's time to take an aggressive approach toward cutting your insurance bill. The best way to do that is to reexamine all your insurance needs.

Begin with health insurance. Bear in mind the real

reason for having medical coverage: to provide a safety net in case of a catastrophe. You don't need medical insurance coverage for an annual physical that costs $200. Its purpose is to pay for expenses you cannot cover yourself. That's why you should calculate how large a deductible you can afford—in effect becoming as much of a self-insurer as possible. If you and your significant other can afford to absorb $1,000 in medical bills each, increase the deductible to that level. The higher the deductible you take, the lower your monthly premium will be.

Similarly, consider alternative types of coverage. In the traditional form of coverage, called major medical, the insured has complete control over physician selection and, after meeting the deductible, generally receives reimbursement for 100 percent of all costs. But in exchange for this freedom and total coverage you pay a higher premium. Costs can be reduced somewhat by incorporating a coinsurance element into major medical: Coverage is limited to a percentage of claims up to a certain dollar threshold when it becomes total.

Two even more affordable alternatives are health maintenance organizations and health insurance plans. Under these alternative systems the insured is required to use the services of participating physicians, and in return, costs and premiums are reduced. The drawback of course is that your options are limited. A possible compromise type of plan has recently emerged called a preferred provider organization. Under this system the insurance company allows and covers visits to any physician but pays a greater percentage of the cost if a participating physician is used.

Life insurance in America is often more closely linked to ego than to need. We mistakenly believe that buying life insurance is the equivalent of setting a

value on our life. Most of us have far more life insurance coverage than we need. To begin with, if you
don't have dependents, you don't need life insurance.
If you do have dependents, you only need enough life
insurance to pay off debts; cover funeral expenses; take
care of outstanding obligations—a child's college education, for example; and to provide your significant
others with enough money to replace your income for
two to three years, at which time they'll either have
increased their own income or changed their life-style.
Any benefit larger than the sum of these costs is unnecessary. Also, forget about all the variations that agents
offer, such as whole, variable, and universal life. You're
buying insurance, not making an investment. Stick
with term life insurance. It's cheapest and offers the
best coverage.

Next examine your disability insurance coverage.
If you don't have any, get some as soon as possible. It's
expensive but far more important even than life insurance. You've a four times greater chance of becoming
disabled between the ages of thirty-five and sixty than
of dying. Many people make the mistake of taking out
a policy that pays a benefit equal to their gross income.
Benefits on disability policies for which you pay the
premium are tax free. That means you only need to receive your take-home pay. In addition, assume that if
you become disabled, you'll be changing your life-style
and spending less, thus lowering the necessary benefit
even farther. Finally try to increase the amount of time
between when you become disabled and when benefits
start. This is the equivalent of boosting a deductible. If
you've four months' worth of expenses already saved
and your company provides three months of disability
coverage, you don't need your benefits to start until
after you've been disabled for seven months.

Homeowner's insurance can also be trimmed to

save money. Remember, the purpose of your insurance is to rebuild your home in case of disaster, not to replace a broken window—so take as high a deductible as you can afford. Change your policy to only cover the existing structure, not the surrounding property. The land your home sits on can't be destroyed by a fire. Next, go through your personal-property coverage with a fine-tooth comb. Only carry insurance on those items that you can or would replace if lost or damaged. There's no way you could ever replace your great grandmother's earrings, so why insure them?

Finally, take a close look at your auto insurance coverage. While a certain amount of coverage is required by many states, policies usually cover more than this minimum amount. Pare back coverage as close to the state requirements as possible. If your car is more than three years old, eliminate collision coverage. Check the list of regular drivers of the car. If your teenage son or daughter just went away to college, scratch his or her name off the policy. Make sure you aren't paying for duplicate coverages. Some people pay auto club membership fees and at the same time unwittingly continue to pay for towing coverage on their auto insurance. In addition some homeowner's policies may also cover items stolen from your vehicle, eliminating the need for your auto policy to do the same.

Trimming your insurance coverage in this manner can result in an annual savings of one to two months' worth of expenses. Added to your debt-reduction efforts, this should bring your cash reserve up to between three and five months' worth of money. Coming up with the remainder is where it starts getting tough.

Take out your checkbook and start calculating how much you money you actually spend each month and how much can be eliminated. It's time to streamline and simplify your life-style in an effort to save money.

Can you take mass transportation rather than driving or taking a cab? Couldn't you launder and iron your own shirts rather than going to the dry cleaner? Start buying clothes on an as-needed basis rather than by the season. Have hemlines and lapels changed and shoes resoled.

How many times do you eat out each month? Cut it down to once a month, at most, don't overtip, and have coffee and dessert at home. Rather than buying books, why not go the library? Instead of going to the movies once a week, rent a videotape and make your own popcorn. Brown-bag it rather than going out to lunch. Buy magazines at the newsstand rather than subscribing—you'll spend less and end up reading more. Slice your gift giving in half. There's no rule that gifts must increase in value each year. Consider giving baked goods or handmade items at the holidays—people will be thrilled.

Try your best to become a savvy shopper. Clip coupons and prepare a list before you go food shopping. When you get to the supermarket, buy generic, store, or regional brands rather than heavily advertised national products. Compare unit prices. Buy staples in bulk. Limit your mail-order shopping to discount catalogs, not boutique brochures. Use the telephone to get price quotes from a variety of stores when buying an expensive item, and then go directly to the retailer who has the cheapest price. Stop browsing: Shopping should be a chore, not a hobby.

Cut down on your telephone and utility bills. Place egg timers by the telephone to remind you to keep calls short. Turn thermostats down to 50 degrees when you leave the house in the morning and down to 60 when you go to bed at night. Turn lights out when you leave a room. If you've an electric range, turn the burner off a minute or two before the food is done. The coil will

remain hot long enough to finish the job. Fill the dish-
washer completely before running it and use energy-
saving settings whenever possible. Wash clothes in
cold rather than warm or hot water and line-dry them.
It costs nothing and they end up smelling fresh and
clean. Take showers instead of baths—they use less
water.

I'm sure you already knew about most of these money-
saving devices. They're the tactics our parents learned
and lived by when times were tough and money was
tight. In the past ten years, however, we put all this
behind us. As the economy boomed, whatever frugality
we had absorbed in our youth was thrown out the window. We bought into the disposable, credit-oriented so-
ciety. Instant gratification was too slow. But in order
to come out of this recession, we need to practice a little bit of old-fashioned thrift. I'm not saying you must
follow all the tips I've outlined above and start living
like a monk or a miser. But you've got to stop living
only for today and start living for tomorrow as well.
By streamlining your debts, trimming your insurance
premiums, and cutting back on your monthly expenses
you can set aside the six months' cash reserve you need
to truly be safe during this recession. It won't be easy,
but it has to be done.

TOTAL INDEBTEDNESS WORK SHEET

Column 1 Name and Type of Loan	Column 2 Balance Due	Column 3 Interest Rate	Column 4 Monthly Payment

Total of column 2 equals total indebtedness   _____

Total of column 4 equals monthly debt service   _____

MORTGAGE REFINANCING WORK SHEET

Section A—Potential Savings

1. Current monthly payment _____
2. New monthly payment _____
3. Line 2 subtracted from line 1
   equals potential monthly savings _____
4. Line 3 multiplied by 12 equals
   potential yearly savings _____
5. Line 4 multiplied by term of loan
   equals total potential savings _____

Section B—Cost of Refinancing

6. Cost of up-front points _____
7. Bank's attorney's fees _____
8. Your attorney's fees _____
9. Bank's application and appraisal fees _____
10. Total of lines 6, 7, 8, and 9 equals
    total cost of financing

Section C—Break Even

11. Line 10 divided by line 3 equals
    number of months it takes to break
    even _____

CHAPTER 6

Cutting Your Income Tax Bill

It was as true . . . as turnips is.
It was as true . . . as taxes is.
And nothing's truer than them.
—Charles Dickens

You probably spend more money on taxes than anything other than shelter. Depending on where you live and how much you earn, from 15 to 43 percent of your income goes straight to Uncle Sam and your local taxing authority. Yet few Americans do much about it.

The American approach to taxes is much like our laissez-faire attitude toward health care. We treat rather than prevent. Every March you sit down with a tax preparer and try to figure out ways to minimize the damage the IRS has already done to your bank account. You complain, play around with the numbers, and perhaps even manufacture a few deductions. But after April passes, you return to a state of blissful ignorance, ignoring the steady tax drain on your dollar and even using potential tax deductibility as a rationale for making unnecessary purchases.

It's time for this neglect to stop. In a recession no expense can be ignored—especially not one that takes more than a third of your income. And rather than relying on last-minute surgery, it's time to start practicing year-round preventive medicine. That means enacting an ongoing and constant program of aggressive tax planning and avoidance. Such a program is perhaps the single best way to cut expenses in a recession, since it requires little work, few sacrifices, and can result in enormous savings.

Instead of relying on a neighbor's advice, a storefront tax preparer, or the latest paperback tax guide, get some professional guidance. Don't even think of depending on the IRS technical-assistance hot line. The idea behind it is great—but the execution isn't: Up to one-third of the answers given are wrong, according to some independent audits. You need a certified public accountant. Not only are CPAs licensed and therefore fully accountable for their actions, most are also year-round tax consultants. And from this point on, tax avoidance is going to be a part of our daily lives, not just something we do in the spring.

Ask your other financial professionals to recommend CPAs for you to interview. Bankers, attorneys, and financial planners deal with CPAs on a regular basis and should know who's sharp and who's not. While large firms can offer more services, I prefer small firms or sole proprietors. They're just as qualified, their fees are substantially lower, and they provide a much more personalized service. I like to be able to pick up the telephone and ask my accountant a question without having to cut through four layers of bureaucracy.

Telephone all the CPAs on your list and schedule appointments to meet with them in their office. Make sure to bring along your three most recent tax returns and, if you're in business for yourself, the past year's financial statements. Ask if the CPA has other clients in occupations similar to your own. You don't want to be a CPA's guinea pig. It's a plus if he's a member of the American Institute of Certified Public Accountants, but it's more important he takes classes and seminars on a regular basis. Tax regulations change nearly every year, so savvy CPAs are always taking courses. Ask each one to characterize his approach to tax avoidance—is he conservative or aggressive—and make sure it matches your own philosophy. In this recession I advise you to err on the side of aggressiveness. Don't be afraid to ask about and negotiate the accountant's fee. While they range from $75 to $200 per hour, accountants are in a recession as well and may be willing to cut their profit to bring in added cash. When selecting an accountant the final factor to consider is how he or she will appear to an IRS agent. While your chances of actually being audited are slim—even when practicing aggressive avoidance—you want to make sure the accountant who would be sitting next to you in an IRS office would be an effective advocate.

Once you select a CPA, schedule an appointment with her as soon as possible. Plan on working with your CPA at least twice a year: once to plan your tax strategy for the year, and again to prepare your tax return. In addition you'll also contact her if, during the year, anything happens that could affect your tax status. Prior to your first meeting, send the CPA copies of your past several tax returns and any financial inventories you've prepared. Bring brokerage account statements, pension fund information, and your employee handbook with you as well.

During the initial planning meeting the first order of business is making sure you aren't paying too much in estimated taxes or having too much withheld from your paycheck. Review the amounts of your quarterly payments and the number of deductions claimed on your W-4 form with an eye toward eliminating an overpayment. Your goal should be to break even, or owe a little bit, when filing a return. Even though the IRS pays refunds fairly promptly, you've lost potential interest and investment income on those refunded dollars.

Another way of minimizing the impact of taxes on your paycheck is to reexamine the fringe benefits offered by your employer. Many companies today offer cafeteria-type plans, in which employees are allowed to pick and choose from a benefits package including such things as medical insurance, life insurance, disability insurance, dental care, eyeglass coverage, and child-care or elder-care expenses. Since these benefits are paid for with pretaxed dollars, having payment for them withheld rather than actually going through your checking account can save hundreds or even thousands of dollars in the course of a year.

Since, other than a home mortgage, the only tax shelter available to most Americans is a retirement plan, you and the CPA should next figure out how to maximize tax-deductible contributions to these plans. Don't look to your CPA for advice on what particular product or instrument to invest retirement dollars in—such advice should come from a certified financial planner. Simply ask her to determine how much you can actually shelter and then calculate the possible effect on your tax bill.

Your CPA may have suggestions on how to use children to reduce a tax bill. Under the Uniform Gift to Minors Act, children under the age of fourteen only need pay $75 in taxes on gift income of up to $1,000. If you were to hold on to the $1,000, the tax on it could be as high as $310. By giving the money to your child there's an effective tax savings of up to $235 for each gift. Individuals in business for themselves can also shift money into a lower tax bracket by paying a salary to their fourteen-year-old or younger children. If this business isn't incorporated, it won't even need to pay employment taxes on the salaries.

Individuals with solid cash flow should speak with their accountant about possibly using savings to pay down mortgages. For example, if you have a nontax-deductible 11 percent mortgage, it makes sense to take money that's earning 8 percent interest out of the bank and use it to reduce your mortgage debt. In effect you'll have increased the effective yield of the money from 8 to 11 percent. If your mortgage *is* tax deductible, have the CPA do a cost-benefit analysis to see if reducing the debt makes sense. Similarly owners of second homes that are rental properties may be able to reduce nondeductible passive losses—which result when the monthly mortgage payment is higher than the monthly rent—by paying down their mortgages from personal savings.

Finally ask your accountant to design a record-keeping system for you. Meticulous records that allow for nearly instant summarizing can cut the amount of time the accountant must spend preparing the return, thus lowering his or her fee and trimming even more from your tax bill. Once you understand the accountant's preferred record-keeping system, the agenda for the meeting is completed. You won't need to schedule another until tax time, unless of course something financially significant happens in the interim.

There's no more financially significant event than loss of a job, and a CPA's advice can help minimize the financial pain. Your accountant can offer guidance on whether or not you should take early pension plan distributions or hardship withdrawals from 401K plans. A savvy CPA should also be able to quickly determine whether severance should be taken immediately or deferred until the next tax year, when you may be in a lower bracket due to reduced income. A CPA can also tell you which job-hunting and job-relocation expenses are tax deductible.

If you receive notification from the IRS that you owe back taxes, contact your CPA immediately. They can help clear up the mistake if there is one, negotiate an installment payment plan if there isn't, and tell you whom to pay first if more than one agency has discovered the mistake. They'll also be able to help you keep your money out of the reach of the IRS collection computer so that you can earn interest on it, without resorting to misrepresentation.

Whenever you're about to make a large purchase or receive a sizable chunk of income toward the end of the year, speak with your CPA first. They'll be able to determine whether it's better to take the expenses and/or income this year or to wait until next.

No event has more of a taxable impact than the sale of a home; that's why your CPA should be among the first you let know of your intention to sell. Advance planning can minimize the taxes on a sizable profit, or turn a loss into a tax deduction. If you expect to make a profit on the sale of a home, a CPA can help implement the two-year rollover rule, which allows you to defer payment of capital gains taxes if you're under fifty-five, or prepare you to take the lifetime exclusion of up to $125,000 in profit if you're over fifty-five. Normally a loss on the sale of a personal residence would not be tax deductible. But if you expect a loss and contact your CPA early enough, she can help convert the home into a rental property, which will then let you deduct the sale as a business loss. The only catch is that the IRS will let you deduct only whichever is lower: its value at the time of conversion or the current market value.

Barring any of these situations, you'll next be

meeting with your CPA in late February or early March to prepare your tax return. The two of you will go over your deductions for the year. Astute CPAs will compare your deductions with those claimed by other Americans in the same tax bracket. Any deduction that appears out of character for your income could trigger an audit, especially since the demise of tax-sheltered investments has left IRS investigators with lots more time on their hands. Your CPA will know which deductions should be accompanied by documentation in order to nip audit notices in the bud.

She'll also be able to preempt some penalty notices. For example, if you owe more than 10 percent of what you paid in estimated taxes, an automatic penalty notice will be spit out by the IRS computer. However, there are quite a few exemptions to this penalty, including having paid in estimated taxes a sum equal to your previous year's total tax. Rather than waiting for the penalty notice to arrive, a smart CPA will include the explanatory form with the return itself.

Most CPAs do neat and accurate work, but it's still important for you to do some final proofreading before mailing the returns. First make sure all the arithmetic is correct. Next make sure every person claimed as a deduction has a Social Security number, and that both you and your CPA have signed and dated the return. Finally send your tax returns by certified mail, return receipt requested. That way you'll have proof they were mailed on time if the IRS mistakenly claims they were filed late and demands a penalty.

PART II

FIGHTING FOR YOUR LIFE

*Never give in, never give in, never, never, never, never—
in nothing, great or small, large or petty—
never give in except to convictions of honor and good
sense.*
—Sir Winston Spencer Churchill

CHAPTER 7

*Appealing a Layoff and
Negotiating Severance*

The gods help them that help themselves.
—Aesop

I'm afraid it's too late for some people to renew their job vows. As each day passes, it's becoming clearer that a great many more Americans will lose their jobs during this recession. While every employee who has ever been laid off is angry and fearful, those hit by this round of firings will be particularly devastated. First, it's taking place during a recession, when their personal finances are already being buffeted. Most will be white- and gold-collar workers and professionals who never assumed they'd experience unemployment. And they're being thrust into a job market that has literally hundreds of qualified—and desperate—candidates for each opening. Recent studies indicate it's taking white-collar workers between six and seven months to find a job that pays the same as their previous position. That's why if you get called down to the personnel office at 4:00 P.M. on a Friday, you must be prepared to stage the negotiation of your life.

Once the dreaded words "your services are no longer required" are spoken, get a tight grip on your emotions. Even though your blood is boiling and the tears are welling up, remain calm. If you don't feel you can contain your emotions, ask for an adjournment—most employers and almost all personnel executives will agree. Visible anger and sorrow are, at this point, counterproductive. You probably had some inkling this was going to happen—firings and layoffs are rarely surprises. Management generally gives warnings, cautions, and hints well in advance of actually dropping the ax in order to avoid emotional scenes later on. You see, they're extremely scared about firing people.

Anyone who has ever had to fire an employee knows how uncomfortable it is to do. If it's for a just cause—they stole from the company, for instance—the executioner's personal feelings are kept under a blanket of righteous indignation. But if it's a firing at will—you're not working up to par or there's a need to cut costs—the executioner feels tremendous anxiety. Across the desk sits not just the employee but his or her family as well. Visions of *A Christmas Carol* come to mind. Suddenly the employee becomes Bob Cratchit, father to little crippled Tiny Tim, and the one doing the firing becomes mean and cruel Ebenezer Scrooge. Or the employee becomes a symbol of an entire minority group who can lead a long, costly, and public legal battle over wrongful termination. And lurking in the mind of every executive who must fire someone is the fear that the employee may become abusive or violent.

While I wasn't afraid of her becoming violent, I was terribly concerned about having to fire my bookkeeper this year. Even though the decision was purely economic and couldn't be avoided, I felt like a heel. It was as if I was taking bread out of the mouths of her children. My associate and office manager was so upset by the whole process that she had to leave the office while it was being done.

The hope and dream of every executioner is for the condemned to accept her fate gracefully, as thankfully, my bookkeeper did. His nightmare is the person who gets physical and goes down kicking and screaming; the employee who trashes files, sabotages customer relations, destroys company morale, or who claims discrimination and takes the employer to court. Realizing this gives you, the employee, tremendous leverage. In fact you've never been more powerful at this job. The only real leverage an employer has over an employee is the threat of termination. Once the threat has been acted on, there's nothing more he or she can do to you. Employers are like armies with a single, very powerful cannon. If they don't crush your spirit by firing the big gun, the advantage shifts to you.

Since you've taken their best shot and, hopefully, haven't exploded in rage or collapsed in grief, you can go on the offensive. But before that's possible, you need to find out why you've been fired. Generally employees are fired for either economic or personal reasons. An economic firing is when a department is eliminated because it's not profitable, there has been a merger and positions have become redundant, or individual positions are eliminated in order to save money. Personal reasons can be that you didn't get along with co-workers, your performance wasn't up to desired standards, your attendance was poor, or your supervisor didn't like you. Whether or not you agree with the reason given, unless you're a member of a minority group, it's the one you must work with.

The first phase of your offensive is to try to get a reconsideration of the firing. I'm not suggesting you stay with a company that is willing to fire you—I think you need to go elsewhere. But remember, we're in a recession. While it's possible to get a job during a recession, the economic pressures make it difficult to hold out long enough to find something worthwhile. And it's always easier to find a job when you're still employed. Reconsideration, if successful, provides you with the time to look for, and improves your chances of finding, a better job. Getting a decision reversed isn't impossible. There's a reverence for the appellate process in America, which even extends to employers and personnel executives. In order to maximize the chances of being "unfired," it's vital that you counter the reason for the firing and offer the employer a way to save face.

When told the layoff is because of economic reasons, respond with the statement "I enjoy working here and really don't want to leave the company." Say you'd be happy to work for another department or branch of the company, even if it means going back for retraining. Explain how your job actually cut across several departments and ask if your salary can be allocated differently, perhaps against other budgets. Tout your skills and abilities. Describe the loyal customer base you've cultivated. In effect, what you're doing is turning the firing meeting into a hiring interview for another position in the company. The guilt generated by firing should be enough to at least get you consideration for any jobs the company has available. Never defuse this guilt by nodding or indicating that you understand your employer's position. Listen stoically and then indicate you'd be willing to discuss a reduction in salary if money is the problem—this gives the employer a convenient way of taking you back and still saving face.

This worked for a client of mine who was told she was being fired from her public relations job for budgetary reasons. Instead of simply accepting the decision, she asked her immediate superior for a reconsideration. When he explained there was nothing he could do, she asked if it was all right to approach the president of the company. He agreed without hesitation. She prefaced her discussion with the company president by saying, "My superior suggested I speak with you." This implied the superior somehow agreed with her appeal but felt his hands were tied. She made her pitch for continued employment to the president, adding the fact that she'd be willing to accept a reduction in salary. The president told her to "try to work things out" with her superior. She returned bearing the president's mandate and the olive branch of a salary reduction. Her immediate superior, feeling the pressure from above and viewing the salary reduction as a way to save face, agreed to the compromise.

When fired for something personal, you must demonstrate contrition. Rather than argue the point, agree with your executioner. Once you've disarmed him, move in for the kill. Say, "This is the best job I've had, and I don't want to lose it." Lay it on thick. Tell him you now understand the problem and can work at correcting it. Say, "I'm not looking for a second chance, just an opportunity to atone for my mistakes." As a face-saving device ask about a probationary period. Contrition works better with supervisors than with personnel executives—those trained in firing are able to eliminate most guilt feelings—so do everything possible to get to someone outside of personnel. Push the "up" button and ask to speak to your immediate superior or her supervisor. The personnel department won't object—that would be like a declaration of war.

If your appeal is granted and results in a reprieve, offer profuse thanks to all, swear your undying loyalty, and then immediately turn to chapter 11 and start looking for another job. If your appeal doesn't work, don't feel as though your effort has been wasted. Employers are so afraid of the firing process that they orchestrate it like a funeral. All the details are taken care of in advance, and you're supposed to just go along with the scenario as if you were a corpse. Asking for reconsideration throws a monkey wrench in their plan. It's as if during a funeral the corpse got up and started asking what was going on. You've effectively disoriented your employer and seized control of the process.

After exhausting all avenues of appeal, concentrate on maximizing your severance package. Rather than relying on guilt, offer the employer a quid pro quo. Say, "While I'm unhappy about it, I can understand your decision. I want you to know I'll do everything I can to help ease the transition." Offer to train your replacement and to work with him or her for a period of time. Graciously suggest you'd be willing to call your loyal customers and reassure them. Signal your willingness to be more than just the docile corpse they were hoping for, to actually help with your own burial. But ask for some help in return for your collaboration.

Ask for a positive reference letter and insist that it be prepared immediately. Don't accept assurances that the company's policy is to respond to all reference inquiries with objective rather than subjective information. Comments such as "we're not at liberty to discuss that," or "we can't get into those matters," amount to being damned with faint praise. Despite claims of it being company policy, callers may feel that something is being hidden from them. If the letter is written now, while guilt feelings are still running high, it's bound to be more positive than if your supervisor has time to think about it, so make sure you've the letter in hand before you leave the premises.

See if you can take an active role in the preparation of your reference letter. Ask that it state that the decision to leave was either yours alone or was mutually agreed upon, regardless of the actual circumstances. This helps both parties maintain reputations and images in the industry. At the very least get them to agree to a ruse in which your actual job circumstances remain confidential for a set period of time.

While the standard severance pay is one month's salary for every year you've worked for the company, there's no formal rule. The only limiting factor is your willingness to ask for more. Feel free to bring the current market conditions and economic situation to the attention of your supervisor in explaining why you'll need more severance. In addition, be sure to ask for accrued vacation, sick, and personal-day pay, as well as a refund of your contributions to the company pension plan. If you work on commission, reach an understanding about which sales were due to your efforts and get an agreement on the commissions still owed you, including a specific mention of when they'll be paid. Try to get the company to buy your stock options or else give you their unvested contributions to a pension plan. If they claim to be eliminating your position, ask to take your equipment with you when you go.

Legally you must be given the option of continuing in the company's health care plan for up to eighteen months at your own expense. Explain to your supervisor how severance pay won't be enough to cover the cost of this insurance coverage, so it would be a big help if the company could continue paying the premiums for a period of time. This is especially true for older employees, who may not be able to get affordable life insurance on their own. Each month of continued coverage you can squeeze out of a former employer is a sizable addition to your severance package.

Never just dismiss continuing your health coverage without first doing some investigation. If you or a member of your family is currently being treated for an ailment, it may not be covered by a subsequent health plan, since it could be categorized as a preexisting condition. Losing coverage for a serious preexisting condition can be devastating financially, so ask for additional time to weigh health coverage decisions.

Push for being allowed continued use of your office while looking for another job. Access to your Rolodex—if you didn't bring it home and photocopy it as I suggested back in chapter 2—the company's library or data base, a copying machine, your computer, a fax machine, and the mail room can dramatically reduce the time and cost of finding another job. Some employers may balk at this—they feel your continued presence is a blow to company morale. Go along with their request to vanish gracefully, but in exchange ask for more money to cover the cost of your job search.

Request outplacement guidance and assistance. If none is available, ask for added severance to help pay for it whether or not you're actually going to use it. That can mean another $8,000 to $10,000 in severance. A company that required you to relocate should be reminded of this and asked to provide financial help in returning to your home, where your personal and career network is stronger.

Whatever you and your former employer agree to in this negotiation, it should be documented in writing. Don't leave the office without either having the signed checks in your hand or a signed memo detailing the terms of your agreement. Your physical presence reinforces and amplifies guilt feelings that could subside overnight. Anything you don't get in writing right then you may not get at all. Be careful to check that there are no noncompetitive clauses hidden in the fine print of your termination agreement. If you find a provision that could keep you from finding another job in the same industry, cross it out before signing.

Members of protected minority groups have another tool in their arsenal. Instead of relying on guilt, they can imply that the firing may be discriminatory. Many employers are using this recession to clean house. Under the guise of economic necessity they're getting rid of "problem" workers. In most cases these are workers who show up late, don't work hard, or who have a poor attitude. But in all too many instances, *problem* means "different." In America today a great many groups can claim protection under discrimination laws. Personnel executives are well aware of how damaging even a groundless wrongful termination suit can be. So if you're not a middle-aged, Protestant, heterosexual, physically able, white male of average weight, you may be able to use your minority status as leverage for an increased severance package.

While it's important to put your suspicions on the record as early as possible, you should be careful not to overstate your case or jump to conclusions. After you're given a reason for the firing, take a moment to consider it. If it appears unjustified, tell the person delivering the news, "I have the feeling I'm being singled out." Using the phrase *singled out* should set off an alarm in the head of the other party. Go on to say you "don't believe there's anything in my personnel file or performance to justify this firing." Request that the meeting be adjourned to allow you time to contact an attorney.

Remain calm and logical throughout this exchange. Don't imply the person sitting on the other side of the desk from you is racist, ageist, or anything else. Simply indicate your concerns in a professional, courteous manner. The other party will almost certainly go along with an adjournment, especially if they're a personnel executive who must meet with a superior right away to explain the potential problem. Supervisors will need to contact their own supervisors for guidance. And owner managers may be anxious to speak with their own attorney.

If, however, the other party is taken aback and responds angrily, using words like *extortion* and *blackmail*, you may must defuse the tension yourself. Say, "It's certainly not my intention to blackmail you. You may not even be conscious of it, but I've read enough about wrongful termination to know this may fall under that category. However, I'm not implying any *conscious* discrimination on your part."

It's important to remember your goal is either to derail the firing process so that you have enough time to find another job or to get as much severance as possible. Now isn't the time to fight for principles. The last thing you or your former employer wants is a court battle. The only people who actually win extended legal fights are the lawyers. Regardless of the outcome, the employer is branded a discriminator and the employee is branded a troublemaker. Once the possibility of wrongful termination is raised, you've upped the ante dramatically, and employers will more than likely be prepared to increase their severance offer.

However, I don't believe you should be the one to make the transition from righteously claiming wrongful termination to negotiating for increased severance. Leave this to an attorney who's an expert at "bridge" language. Your legal adviser should help prepare a memo outlining what you'd be willing to accept in exchange for dropping the matter. Sprinkled throughout the memo should be references to the difficulties you'll have in finding another job and, if possible, the problems you'll face as a "special" person. Use the sample memo on pages 113 to 114 as a guide for doing this subtly.

What should you ask for in this memo? The sky is the limit. Your firing has now truly turned into a negotiation, and this memo is simply an offer. As in any other monetary give-and-take, each side stakes out an extreme position and then together they try to reach common ground somewhere in the middle. You should at least ask for all the suggestions mentioned earlier in this chapter as ways of broadening severance.

When you do reach an agreement with your former employer, have your lawyer configure the package as a settlement of proposed litigation rather than as "severance pay." In that way, since the money you receive is in compensation for an injury you suffered rather than for work provided, it's nontaxable. This instantly increases the value of the settlement by your marginal tax bracket. For example, if you receive a severance package of $100,000 and you're in the 38 percent tax bracket, configuring it as a settlement instantly increases the value of the package to $138,000. Employers should have no problem with this arrangement, but if they voice some concern, your attorney can offer to draft a hold-harmless clause, which will take them off the hook by stating that you alone are responsible for any taxes.

Never feel ashamed of getting laid off or fired. You're not alone. Almost everyone is let go at one time or another, and in this recession there are literally millions of others in the same situation. Because of the sheer number of people losing their jobs for purely economic reasons, head hunters and personnel executives no longer view getting laid off as an indication there's something wrong with you; it's no longer a black mark on your career history. Don't hide the news from family, friends, and peers. They can be invaluable sources of emotional support and potential job leads. No one intelligent is going to lessen his or her opinion of you because you were let go.

Some astute company managers are taking a different approach to cutting labor costs. Rather than laying off employees, they're offering to buy them out of their jobs. These offers generally consist of a combination of added severance pay; a single lump-sum cash payment; an allowance for vocational training or outplacement assistance; continued insurance coverage for a period of time; and a pension sweetener. Buyouts allow the company to trim staff and costs without developing a reputation for laying off employees or leaving itself open to wrongful termination suits. These plans keep up the morale of remaining employees and present an image of benevolence to the outside world.

While being made such an offer is clearly better than just getting fired or laid off, you must determine whether it's an offer or a veiled threat. Find out whether the offer was made across the board to everyone in the company or just to a specific group of employees—perhaps only those in one or two departments or those above the age of fifty. When a buyout offer is targeted to a specific group of employees, it amounts to an early warning. That group has been selected as the place to cut back. Implicit in making the offer therefore is a threat: The alternative to accepting the buyout is getting fired or laid off. On the other hand, if the whole company is presented with the offer, it means the organization is looking to reduce overall numbers, not specific departments or employees.

If you're part of a group that's been specifically targeted, you don't have much choice but to let yourself be bought out. But before you acquiesce to the terms of the plan, speak with your attorney, accountant, and financial planner. Ask for suggestions on possible sweeteners for the deal. Then schedule an appointment with personnel and try to negotiate modifications to the plan based on your professionals' suggestions. The company's buyout plan is nothing more than an offer, even though the threat behind it is obvious. When one party makes an offer, the other party has every right to respond with a counteroffer. Tell the company's representative you've studied the offer, are interested, but would like to discuss some potential changes. Before going into your pitch, assure them you'll keep the specific terms of your deal confidential.

If you're not being specifically targeted, you've more of a chance to weigh the options. Companies always compare buyout offers with what employees would receive if they were fired or laid off, but assuming this offer is actually voluntary, it should really be compared with what you'd get if you stayed on the job. Sit down with your financial advisers and go over the differences. Look at more than just the dollars. How did you feel about your job the day prior to learning of the buyout offer? If you knew your future lay elsewhere, this buyout may be the perfect opportunity to find another job, shift careers, or start your own business. On the other hand, if you were planning to stay with this company until retirement, then why quit now? Buyout offers are always designed to work out economically for the company. Over the long term, employees who remain receive more than those who leave. The decision comes down to whether you really have a choice in the matter and what your plans are for the future.

Whether you've been fired, laid off, or bought out, remain positive. You're in control. If you've followed my suggestions in this chapter, you have some time, so there's no need to panic. Look on this as the opportunity to find a better job, or to shift careers, or to start your own business. In my experience, people who are laid off or fired always end up, in the long term, improving their lives.

Sample Memo Negotiating Terms of Settlement for Potential Wrongful Termination

This is a somewhat edited version of the text of a memo I helped a client prepare in response to being laid off. A sixty-five-year-old experienced middle manager, she suspected the company had singled her out because of age.

Dear Discriminating Employer:

I've discussed the circumstances of your decision to terminate my employment and the severance terms offered with my attorney. I believe, considering my age and the length and quality of my service to the company, the proposed package is inadequate and even unfair in a number of areas.

I believe a serious effort should be made to place me in another division of the company. My experience, skills, and training are valuable to the organization. I'm in excellent health, am ready, willing, and able to continue my career, and am willing to go through retraining if necessary.

If I'm not absorbed into another division, I'll be forced into the job market. At my age it will be difficult to find an equivalent job. Therefore I believe outplacement assistance is called for.

Even with such assistance I may be forced to consider retirement. But under the terms of your offer the monthly benefit I would receive is nowhere near sufficient to maintain my standard of living. I would need at least twice the monthly benefit offered to keep my head above water.

Your offer to me does not include continuation of my life insurance policy. My husband and I are the same age and both contribute financially to our living expenses. If I die before him, without adequate insurance coverage he won't be able to maintain his life-style. My sole life insurance coverage was the policy provided by the company. Now, at age sixty-five, I cannot even buy my own term policy. Therefore, I believe it's only fair that my life insurance coverage be continued if I'm terminated.

If I am indeed forced to leave the company and am unable to find an equivalent job, free-lancing may be my only alternative. In that case I'll need equipment similar to what I now use. Since my position is being completely eliminated, and the equipment will not be needed for a replacement, I expect to be able to take it with me.

In addition, you mentioned that my services as a free-lance consultant will be needed later in the year. I think it reasonable, then, to agree contractually to a set volume and pay level commensurate with my skill and experience.

I look forward to hearing from you.

Sincerely,

Aggrieved Employee

GETTING-FIRED FLOW CHART

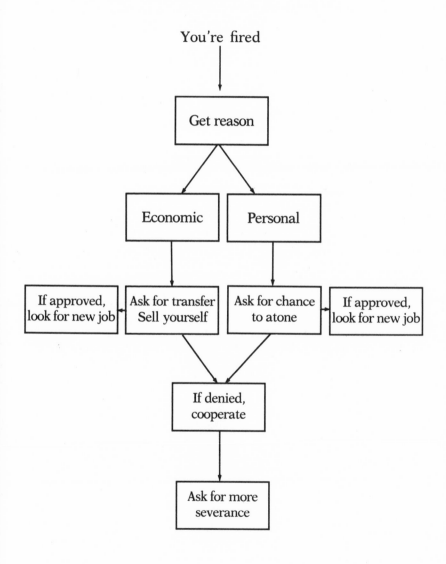

CHAPTER 8

Dealing with Unemployment

"People don't look for kinds of work anymore, ma'am,"
he answered impassively. "They just look for work."
—Ayn Rand

After squeezing every last dollar of severance from a former employer you'll probably feel exhilarated. Exacting a pound of flesh helps satiate the longing for employer blood. But the satisfaction lasts but a few short hours. However large a severance package you've negotiated, in the final analysis it doesn't compensate for being fired.

Self-worth and career are irrevocably linked in America. Our job is a large part of the foundation of our lives. The image we project to others, as well as our self-image, are both based to a large degree on what we do for a living. When asked to describe yourself, what's the first thing you say? I'll bet you mention job before marital status, children, residence, or anything else. Everyone does. It's not that we place more importance on career than on family—though some surely do. It's just that occupation is a clearer definition of who we are. Lots of people are married or single or live in a particular place. Fewer are accountants, or teachers, or house painters, or film projectionists.

When this keystone is removed, the whole structure of your life appears to be on the verge of crumbling. That's understandable: You spend more time at a place of business and with co-workers than at home with family. Suddenly you've no place to go and nothing to do. And what's worse, the defining factor of your life has vanished. It's as if you've become a nonperson. At first you'll feel completely disoriented. Then you'll get angry at your employer and yourself. Depression sets in next. And perhaps after a period of time you'll come around to accepting the situation.

What's happening is that you're going through a period of mourning. These are the same emotional stages people go through when grieving for a lost loved one. I don't mean to equate the loss of a job with the loss of a person. But for those who have never dealt with death before, the loss of a job is the most devastating and traumatic event they've ever experienced. Every religion and culture has developed rituals to help those who have lost a loved one move through the stages of mourning. But there's no ritualized mourning period for losing a job. Rather than being able to fall back on your faith or heritage in a time of personal catastrophe, you end up in a free-fall.

In order to keep from plummeting to the depths of depression, you need to reach out for a support system—your friends and family. One of the most embarrassing and painful things in the world is telling family and friends you've lost your job. You wonder what they'll think of you and you berate yourself for "letting them down." Yet despite any feelings of shame, you must tell people. In this time of grief you need support from those who love you and have faith in you. Hiding the truth of your situation is pitiful, not brave.

Rein in your desire immediately to jump back into the saddle. Even if you've been a go-getter all your life, don't pick up the telephone and start networking right away. Those who have just been fired are in no position to sell themselves. All the pain, anger, self-pity, and resentment you're feeling are bound to show up in your conversations with business associates. Pick up the telephone now and you'll project the self-doubt of a Woody Allen when you want to radiate the self-confidence of a Kennedy. Don't worry about getting bored. As you'll see, there's a lot to do.

Take some time off to mourn your job loss. I'm not saying go to the Caribbean for a month—you're grieving, not celebrating. Just take a few days or a couple of weeks to spread the word among your family and friends and to give yourself time to work through your feelings of anger and resentment. How long this will take depends on how closely linked were your self-image and your job. Those who have had tragedies in their lives, who have experienced ups and downs, will probably come through the grief period quicker than those who have never had a setback before. But trust me, everyone gets over it eventually. Once you've had a chance to mourn, you'll be able to start putting the pieces of your life back together.

Before actually starting the reconstruction, however, you need to figure out how long you've got to do it. That means taking a complete financial inventory while you're grieving. You can do this yourself, but if you have a financial planner or accountant, or if one is being provided as part of your severance package, enlist his or her help in this process.

Begin by simply listing all your assets. Take out a piece of paper and divide it into three columns. If you prefer, you can use the work sheet on pages 130 to 131. In the first column list the actual monetary value of all your assets. Begin with the balances of your bank accounts, making sure to include your severance pay.

Next tabulate the current value of investments, such as savings bonds, life insurance policies with cash values, stocks, bonds, mutual funds, annuities, and other securities. Include in the list any monies you're owed. Write down the market value of your home and other real estate holdings. Finally list the resale value of all your valuable possessions, from cars and collectibles to furs and furniture. Remember to be as realistic as possible in coming up with market and resale values. This financial statement is for your use only, so it makes no sense to inflate numbers for egotistical purposes.

Next, in the second column, compile a list of how much income you can expect each month. Include the monthly take-home pay from your significant other's job and any other regular sources of money, such as gifts or stock dividends. If you can borrow money from a relative or friend each month, include it as well. Calculate how much interest you'll earn each month on investments and savings, making sure to add the severance pay to the principal.

Finally, in the third column, prepare a list of your monthly expenses. Include mortgage or rent payments, taxes, food, utilities and telephone charges, insurance premiums, household maintenance costs, auto expenses, loan payments, and nonrefundable medical bills. Use this analysis as a time to prune monthly costs to the bone. From this moment on, you're on an austerity budget. Forget about clothing purchases, entertainment, recreation, and charitable contributions. It's going to take some time to find another job during this recession, so it's vital to stretch money as far as possible. (For more information on emergency finances, read chapter 9.)

Examine your numbers with an eye toward determining how long you can stay afloat without a steady stream of income from a job. Start by comparing monthly income to monthly expenses. If the remaining income is equal to or greater than the monthly expenses, you're in great shape. Unfortunately few people are so lucky. If monthly expenses are greater than monthly income, you must either borrow money or dispose of assets in order to pay the bills.

Categorize your assets into those readily available to meet expenses (such as cash in bank accounts); those you wouldn't mind converting into cash (such as dormant valuable possessions and collectibles); those you'd be willing to convert if you had to (investments and pension plans, for example); and those you'd be loath to part with (your home, furnishings, and valued personal possessions). Divide the total of each category by the difference between monthly income and expenses, in order to determine how many months' expenses you'll be able to gain by selling each type of asset.

Let's say your significant other has a monthly income of $1,000. After trimming and tabulating, you determine you have monthly expenses of $3,000, leaving you $2,000 in the red each month. Meanwhile you categorize your assets and find you have the following: $12,000 in bank accounts; $2,000 worth of dormant possessions and collectibles; $6,000 available in investments and pension funds; and $200,000 worth of assets you don't want to give up. That means you can live off your bank accounts for six months ($12,000 ÷ $2,000 = six months). If you sell your dormant possessions and collectibles, you can stretch it for another month ($2,000 ÷ $2,000 = one month). And if necessary, you can make it another three months by selling investments and dissolving the pension plan ($6,000 ÷ $2,000 = three months). All this means you have ten months (6 + 1 + 3 = 10) to find a job before you may be forced to sell your home. Don't look on this as simply calculating a worst-case scenario. It's more of a guide to how discriminating you can be in looking for a job. In this example you'd probably feel free to be discriminating for up to six months, feel a little less choosy in the seventh, and get downright desperate in the eighth. Incidentally don't hesitate to liquidate assets just because it might require you to pay taxes. At this point tax considerations are secondary.

After doing all your financial calculations, get a copy of your credit report. More and more employers today are checking the credit histories of job candidates, believing they're indicative of character. So before you even think about going back into the job market, you must clean up your credit file. Correct any mistakes you find and try to get negative comments about your past history changed. If you discover a particular creditor has characterized you as a slow payer or as being in default, contact them directly and ask for the assessment to be changed, perhaps in exchange for complete payment of any outstanding balance. If you're unable to completely clean up the report, prepare a 100-word statement to be included in your file, offering a legitimate explanation of past problems. Medical problems or family emergencies are the best excuses.

With your financial inventory is complete, it's time to conduct a personal inventory. The first part of this analysis is to find out why you were terminated. I know, that was the first thing you asked as soon as your employer dropped the bombshell. But give some thought to whether or not he gave you their real reason. Employers, even during a recession, make every effort to retain exceptional employees. Let's face it: Unless you worked for a large company that made a strictly economic decision to cut a department, you were singled out for some reason. In some cases it could have been for a reason beyond your control, such as seniority, race, age, gender, ethnic background, or religion. But maybe, just maybe, you could have done something about it.

I don't believe in blaming the victim, but think back to chapter 2, in which I explained how we tend to grow complacent on a job; how we lose the spark and enthusiasm that went along with the pressures of being a new employee. Perhaps you started coming to work a bit late and leaving early. Maybe you stopped trying to improve things and instead shifted into neutral. It's possible your appearance started to suffer along with your attitude. Or could it be that you were bored or angry and stopped trying to hide it? Actually it might have been a combination of all these factors. Separately they mean little, but taken together they paint the picture of an employee who's likely to be laid off it there's a choice.

It's highly unlikely an employer will come right out and tell an employee she's being fired because of these minor factors. It's much easier to dismiss her with an innocuous cliché, such as "you weren't right for the job," or to blame it all on the numbers. And being able to spot these traits in yourself is very difficult—how many of us can actually look in the mirror and see an accurate reflection of ourselves? Instead turn to your significant other, a former co-worker, family, or friends for guidance on what went wrong. Ask for a totally honest appraisal of your work attitude and appearance. Explain you're counting on them to be blunt because you've nowhere else to turn for help. Don't get angry or disagree with their assessment. Hold your tongue, listen, and learn.

Fifteen years ago I was under contract with a major bank, serving as their senior real estate consultant. It was a good job, and I thought I was doing well, until

the president of the bank called me into his office and
said my contract wouldn't be renewed. I was crushed.
For the life of me I couldn't figure out what I had done
wrong. Then it dawned on me to ask my wife. At first
she was reticent, but after I insisted she be brutally
honest, the truth emerged. She had noticed over the
past year I had been waking up later and later and
coming home from the office earlier and earlier. I had
stopped shining my shoes every Sunday night and
wearing only freshly pressed suits. She told me I
seemed to have lost my zeal. She was right on all
counts.

The second part of this personal inventory is easier
to do. Simply list what you liked and disliked about
your job. Be as specific as possible. For example, when
I was with the bank, I liked negotiating with developers but disliked having to do detailed financial analy-
ses of their loan proposals. I believe we do best what
we like most, and like most what we do best. Therefore
the simple listing of likes and dislikes also indicates
what you excel at. You may well find that the aspects
of your job that you enjoyed most, and did best, were
actually on the fringe, or even outside, of your formal
job description. That could well account for your becoming complacent or bored. In order to avoid repeating the same mistake, you're going to use this list
in deciding what you'll do next.

Don't reflexively try to rejoin your prior career
path. While it may seem the sensible step, that doesn't
mean it's the right move. This could be an opportunity
to do something dramatic with your life. Back when
you first chose a job or career path, you based the decision on a perception that it would help you achieve
your goals. Today your goals and perceptions may be
different. Carefully study the list of what you liked and
disliked about your job. And rethink goals in light of

where you are now and which careers offer the best opportunities today. For a list of careers with excellent prospects for the near future, see page 133. Let's look at how this process worked when three different clients of mine found themselves unemployed.

Helen had been a legal secretary for more than thirty years when she was laid off from a midsized law firm. When she was young, women had fewer career options than they do today: They became either nurses, teachers, or secretaries. Even though she hated being treated like a slave by some of the attorneys, she loved helping out with legal research whenever she could. Then one day last fall she was told to clear out her desk. The firm was cutting back, and, according to the partner who delivered the death blow, Helen wasn't sufficiently respectful to the young associates.

Instead of immediately pounding the pavement for another legal-secretary position, Helen considered her options, likes, and dislikes. Money was no longer the compelling factor in staying on the job. Through the years she and her husband had put together a nice little nest egg. In fact her husband was about to retire. While she wasn't ready to retire, she wasn't looking forward to another secretarial job. Her love was legal research, not typing and taking messages. Helen and her husband decided to move down south to the area where they had always planned to retire. Rather than leaving the work force, Helen chose to enter a paralegal training program at a local college. After graduating she took a job at a small law firm located near her new home.

John entered investment banking directly out of graduate school at the age of twenty-five. He had just gotten married, and his goals then were simple. He wanted to be able to afford the best for his wife and the family they were planning. That meant a fine apartment in a nice part of New York City, a weekend home in the country, private school for the children, vacations twice a year, and enough extra money for them to dress well and dine out often. Investment banking was his ticket to riches, he thought. He sacrificed a great deal of his private life in exchange for high pressure, a big salary, and yearly bonuses. But after fifteen years in the business, John was laid off when his company dissolved his whole department.

Rather than immediately looking for another investment banking job, John rethought his goals. He was forty years old and seemed to have achieved much of his youthful dreams. The apartment in the city and the home in the country were already his. He had been able to put his two children through private elementary school. Why go back to the pressure cooker? He felt he had achieved his youthful ambitions and now wanted to pursue a new series of more mature goals—starting his own business and getting to know his children. After some long, heartfelt talks with his wife, John decided to make a change in his life. He and his wife sold their apartment in the city and moved to the country full-time. They enrolled their two children in public junior high school. Using the proceeds from the sale of their apartment, John started his own home-based consulting business. When last I spoke with him, he was ecstatic—even though he wasn't earning half the salary he had made as an investment banker.

Victoria moved to New York City from Colorado four years ago. A journalism major in college, she had always dreamed of working for a major magazine. After slaving for a couple of years on the staff of a trade journal headquartered in Denver, she applied for, and got, a junior staff position on a well-known women's magazine. For four years she worked hard, made contacts, and learned the business. Then one day last summer the editor-in-chief called a staff meeting. It was announced the magazine had been purchased by an international publishing company. Assurances were made to everyone, and talk of "deeper pockets" was everywhere. Yet little more than two months later Victoria and ten other junior editors were told to clear out their desks. A new editor had been named, and she wanted to bring in her own staff.

Crushed, Victoria considered moving back west or looking for a job in a more stable industry. But after talking with her family and friends she realized her goals hadn't changed. Even though it's low-paying, insecure, and high-pressured, she loved magazine work. And with four years of experience she was in a better position to achieve her goals than before. She cut back on her spending, borrowed some money from her parents, took out her Rolodex, and began making telephone calls. Five months later she landed a job on another women's magazine.

Losing your job is actually an opportunity. While it's painful and potentially devastating, it also affords you the chance to rethink your life goals. Look on it as an enforced period of introspection. We are all so caught up in our lives and our careers that we seldom give a moment's thought to our actions. The longer we remain on a job, the more we develop tunnel vision. Whenever we feel a twinge of regret, or find our minds wandering to another option, we cut short the contemplation. I've already invested x years in this job, we say to ourselves. Changing careers now wouldn't be prudent, we think. But refocusing on your actual, current goals and pursuing them, even if they take you in a new direction, is actually the most prudent course of all. If you remain in a field that you no longer find rewarding or interesting, I can almost guarantee you

won't progress any farther. By pursuing work you enjoy and do well you'll improve your life immensely. If
that means staying in the same field, by all means do
so. But if it requires shifting careers, or relocating, or
becoming your own boss, do it. Use this time of personal inventory as a chance truly to take charge of your
career and life.

That's what I did when I lost my job at the bank.
Instinctively I tried to continue on the same career
path I'd been traveling. In the midst of my job search
a friend who knew I was also an attorney asked for my
help with a legal problem. I told him to come to my
home and discuss the matter. He in turn recommended
my services to another friend. This little business I was
running from my dining room table began to snowball.
Not only didn't I have time to look for another job, I
soon realized I didn't want one. I thoroughly enjoyed
my home-based consulting business. It was challeng-
ing, financially rewarding, and also gave me more time
to be with my family. I stopped hunting for a job and
devoted all my efforts to the consulting business. It
was the wisest decision I ever made.

With the mourning period over and your financial
and personal inventories completed, it's time to get
back to work. Whether you've decided to look for another job in your field, shift careers, buy a business, or
start one of your own, it's going to be difficult; and you
must be in tip-top shape, physically and emotionally,
to do it well. After you've come to a decision about
what direction you're taking, go directly to your alarm
clock and set it to go off thirty minutes earlier than
when you were working at your job. Get to bed
early—you've got a full day ahead. If you believe in the
power of prayer, say one.

As soon as the alarm goes off, jump out of bed.
Take a cold shower and go through the grooming ritual

you'd follow if "Good Morning America" was going to be visiting your home. Dress neatly, but comfortably. Go through the newspaper while having a light breakfast—read the news and the business section, but put the classified section aside for now. When you've finished reading, take a brisk walk for thirty minutes. Once back home, sit down at your desk or designated work area. If you're going to be starting a business or looking to buy one, jump to chapter 14. If you're going to go back out into the job market, turn to chapter 11.

FINANCIAL INVENTORY WORK SHEET

Assets

Checking account balance $_____
Savings account balance $_____
Certificates of deposit $_____
Other cash in bank $_____
Value of savings bonds $_____
Value of life insurance $_____
Value of mutual funds $_____
Value of stocks $_____
Value of bonds $_____
Value of annuities $_____
Value of other securities $_____
Monies owed you $_____
Value of home $_____
Value of other real estate $_____
Value of car(s) $_____
Value of collectibles $_____
Value of furnishings $_____
Value of furs and jewels $_____
Value of appliances $_____
Value of other possessions $_____

Total assets $_____

Monthly Income

Income from significant other $_____
Income from child $_____
Gift or loan $_____
Stock dividend $_____
Interest income $_____

Total monthly income $_____

Monthly Expenses

Mortgage or rent payment	$_____
Tax payment	$_____
Food cost	$_____
Utilities bill	$_____
Telephone bill	$_____
Insurance premiums	$_____
Household maintenance cost	$_____
Auto expenses	$_____
Loan payments	$_____
Nonrefundable medical costs	$_____
Total monthly expenses	$_____

TIME FRAME ANALYSIS

Monthly Income   _____
Monthly
  Expenses   _____

Monthly Surplus
  or Deficit   _____

Assets readily   ÷ monthly
  available   _____   deficit =   _____
Assets easily   ÷ monthly
  convertible   _____   deficit =   _____
Assets fairly   ÷ monthly
  convertible   _____   deficit =   _____
Assets to be   ÷ monthly
  protected   _____   deficit =   _____

The Twelve Careers with the Best Job Prospects in the 1990s

1. Computer system analysts
2. Doctors
3. Engineers
4. Marketing executives
5. Mathematics graduates
6. Nurses
7. Physical therapists
8. Radiologists
9. Salespeople
10. Science graduates
11. Software designers
12. Teachers

CHAPTER 9

Surviving Financial Emergencies

*For extreme illnesses extreme
treatments are the most fitting.*
—Hippocrates

I'm afraid some of us will end up in dire financial
straits during the recession. Perhaps your effort at
renewing job vows and beginning a cash reserve came
too late; it's possible you overextended yourself in the
1980s when buying a home or starting a business; or
maybe you're the victim of a medical emergency.
Whatever the reason for your money crisis, take heart:
There are ways to overcome financial disaster.

Before I explain the steps you need to take, you
must work on your attitude. You aren't the only person
who has ever been in trouble. There's always been, and
there always will be, a floating segment of the American population that is in financial trouble. At one time
or another almost all of us experience a setback—you've just had the bad luck to have one during
a recession. Your situation isn't a sign you lack moral
fiber or intelligence. It's just a temporary mathemati-
cal problem. You've nothing to be ashamed of. The
only real shame would be in giving up. Keep opening
your mail and answering the telephone—problems

don't go away by themselves. Wake up early, shower, shave, get dressed, and greet the day boldly.

The first thing to do is to make sure you and your family have enough to eat. Draw the maximum cash advances on all your credit cards and use this money to stock your pantry, refrigerator, and freezer. I know the interest rates are astronomical and it's just one more bill you won't be able to pay—but this is an emergency. Besides, you'll feel better knowing you and your loved ones won't go hungry. Stick to nutritional staples. Buy as if you were stocking a fallout shelter, not preparing a dinner party. Steer clear of prepared foods—they're way too expensive. Concentrate instead on things like chopped meat, chicken, bread, canned vegetables, pasta, rice, tuna, and beans. Before you get home from the supermarket, go directly to the bank. Deposit whatever money is left over in your checking account and put the credit cards themselves in your safe-deposit box.

After you finish putting all the food away, compile a list of your creditors and how much you owe each. Rather than waiting for them to figure out you're in trouble, you're going to telephone them. The goal of these calls is to stem your financial hemorrhaging, to slow down or minimize the amount of cash you actually must pay out.

Don't worry about surprising them. Creditors have been gearing up for debtor problems for the past year—they read the papers too. They've reviewed their policies with an eye toward minimizing the number of bad debts they'll need to write off. Customer service representatives have been briefed on what they can offer to people in trouble and have been given increased latitude to make deals.

But before you actually get on the telephone with these individuals, it's important to understand their point of view. A customer service representative or a collection clerk must demonstrate to their supervisor they're on top of situations; they're supposed to know what's happening with your account or loan, why it's happening, and what you're doing about it. By giving them just this information and then staying in touch, you'll make their job easier; in return they'll be more willing to work with you.

Contact your telephone and utility companies first. Say you have a question about your bill. Once you're connected to customer service, introduce yourself and ask for the name of the person you're speaking with. By addressing the other party by name and then following up with the same person all the time, you'll develop a more personal and responsive relationship. Simply say you "want to speak with them about their billing cycles." Demonstrating you know their jargon marks you as intelligent. Explain you've had a financial setback and may be late with your payment this month. Place the onus on yourself and ask what you should be doing. While there's a great deal of regulatory red tape that can be used to delay their cutting off service to you, it's better to keep the relationship from turning antagonistic. Utility and telephone company customer service representatives generally have a great deal of flexibility. If you can get them on your side and keep them there, you'll have a valuable ally. Incidentally neither the telephone nor the utility company report to credit bureaus.

Those who rent their homes should next contact their landlord. This will probably be your most delicate conversation, since tenants have little leverage with landlords. That means you must play for sympathy—even if it means stretching the truth a bit. It's probably not wise to tell your landlord you've lost your job or in any way mismanaged your life. Instead, say you've "had to sidetrack money to take care of a medical emergency in your family." Lay it on as thick as you can. Tell him you "love your apartment" and in the five years you've lived there you've "cared for it as if it were your own." Let him know you've "never had such a fair landlord," and hopefully he realizes he's never had such a good tenant. Humbly say you'll be staying as long as he lets you. While you're buttering him up, bear in mind that, depending on local laws, it could take a landlord up to six months to evict a tenant for nonpayment of rent.

The next creditors to call are credit and charge card companies. Most of the clerks who'll initially field your calls have very little leeway. Just ask them for the rules regarding late payments. Then push the "up" button and ask to speak to their supervisor. Once you've gotten someone with authority on the line, explain you've "had a financial setback." Make sure you get his or her name, and use it during your conversation. Stress that you don't want to cause the company any problems," and you're "very concerned" with keeping your good credit rating. Then ask if you can either skip a complete payment or pay interest charges only. Vow that you won't use the card again until your finances are back to normal, but don't agree to return or destroy it. Working out a repayment plan will minimize the damage done to your credit file. It will be marked "slow payment" rather than the much more serious "nonpayment."

Finally homeowners should contact the bank that holds their mortgage and/or home equity loan. It's all right to put your mortgage or equity lender at the bottom of the list, since they're the most secured and sanguine of all your creditors—they hold either a lien on or a title to your house as collateral. Your banker will actually be the most understanding of all and the most willing to work out an extended- or reduced-payment plan. The last thing bankers ever want is to foreclose on a home loan—especially in a real estate market like this one. They may never be able to recoup their money if they're forced to sell your home after having to hold on to it for a long period of time.

If you have outstanding bills for work done by your professionals, call their offices. Let them know you've had a temporary setback and are unable to pay in full right away. Tell them you'll pay as much as you can each month. If you have an insurance premium coming due, telephone your agent or broker. Be frank about your situation, stress its temporary nature, and then ask her to advance you the premium. When push comes to shove, a good agent or broker should be willing to take a chance in exchange for holding on to a customer—and his commission dollars.

If at any point a creditor beats you to the punch and telephones about a problem with your account, try to turn the conversation around and act as if you initiated the contact. Tell him he's a "very important creditor" and that you've been trying to contact him, or have been afraid to call him. Then shift into your explanation as if you placed the call.

The reason behind all this telephoning is to keep your bills from being sent to a collection agency. As long as you indicate a willingness to pay your debts, and an ability to make token payments, most creditors will refrain from putting you in for collection. Generally collection agencies are used only when payments are three to four months late and there seems to be no other way of collecting the money. Once they give your bill to a collection agency, there's little you or they can do about negotiating payment terms. That doesn't mean you're defenseless against collection agencies, however.

If one of your bills is put in for collection, you'll receive a letter from the collection agency requesting payment. This notice will state the name of the creditor, the amount of the debt, what to do if you believe the bill is in error, and your legal rights. Under federal law collection agencies cannot call at unusual or inconvenient times; threaten or intimidate; hold creditors up to public ridicule; obtain information under false pretenses; make false statements; imply they are government representatives or that you've committed a crime; send any notices that appear to be legal documents from a court or government agency; collect more than what's legally owed; or deposit a postdated check early. If a collection agency does any of these things to you, immediately contact the local offices of the Better Business Bureau and the state attorney general and register a complaint.

When you hang up the telephone after speaking to the last creditor on your list, start thinking of other ways you can slow down the cash leaving your pocket. It's time for you and your family to go on an austerity budget. That means no more restaurants and no more movies. Until your finances bounce back, entertainment will consist of watching television and taking trips to the library. If you can get a refund on dues you've already paid, cancel your memberships in exercise or social clubs. Start using public transportation instead of driving your car. Better yet, walk—that way you'll combine exercise with saving money. Then take your car off the road entirely to save on insurance. Stop giving gifts and making charitable donations until you're back on your feet. If your financial setback falls during the holidays, simply send notes explaining how much the person's love or friendship means to you. And don't turn down any invitations to dinner.

With your creditors on hold and your austerity

budget in place, the next thing to do is to raise as much cash as you can. The secret is to put aside your inhibitions about asking for help and your desire to keep up appearances. Before I get into the various ways you can raise cash, I must give you two words of warning: While effective, these techniques are not painless, and they cannot be used more than once.

First, raid your retirement and pension funds, closing out any IRA or Keogh accounts you've established over the years. (For information on early withdrawals from 401K, IRA, and Keogh plans, see the charts on pages 146 to 148.) Don't feel guilty—it's crazy to keep money locked up until age sixty-five if you're in desperate trouble at age thirty-five, forty-five, or fifty-five. Sure, the penalties are stiff, but at least you'll have some cash in your pocket. Similarly cash in any extraneous life insurance policies or annuities. The only future you can afford to be concerned with right now is tomorrow.

If you need more cash than your retirement funds offered up, turn to your family and friends and ask to borrow money. If your parents or siblings are in a position to help, don't hesitate to ask them out of a misguided sense of shame. In the America of the 1990s the nest stays open long after emancipation. With the economy turning sour, increasing numbers of adult children are temporarily moving back in with their parents because they're experiencing financial troubles. By insisting that the loans include interest and a pay-back plan, like any other business transactions, you can simultaneously keep your dignity intact and offer a good deal to your lender. Be completely flexible and structure the deals to fit the needs of the individual lender.

If an elderly relative has money set aside for you in her estate, ask for the money now. Explain that

you're truly in need and that this would give her the
chance to see her money do some good and you a
chance to thank her for her generosity. An actor client
of mine was in desperate straits a year ago. He hadn't
been able to land a job for over a year and was forced
to use his credit cards to pay for living expenses. When
he could finally borrow no more, he turned to his only
living relative, an elderly uncle living in the Midwest,
for help. His uncle was eager to lend a hand. For years
this retired attorney had been putting money away for
his nephew's inheritance. He had never thought to ask
if the struggling young actor needed help now.

When borrowing isn't sufficient, you must start
selling off assets. First check your files, desks, and bank
vaults for any savings bonds or stock certificates you
may have forgotten about. Next start scouring the
house for objects that may be valuable to collectors—Uncle Henry's stamp collection that's been up in
the attic for years, for example. Then begin going
through your closets, jewelry boxes, and cabinets for
valuable but unused possessions. The crystal and silver
pieces you got as wedding gifts but never used could
be turned into much-needed dollars.

Go through all your possessions and get together
enough merchandise for a yard sale. Keep in mind that
old furniture, toys, housewares, clothes, jewelry, and
china are all being sought out by collectors today.
Don't repair anything—simply dust it all and put up a
sign saying that everything is sold "as is." Remember,
you're not a retail store—you're a person desperately
trying to raise cash. That means your prices must be
flexible. When you originally put price tags on your
wares, first write in a higher price and then cross it off,
indicating your willingness to negotiate. Every thirty
minutes slash the price of items still unsold by 10 percent. If a customer makes a reasonable offer, accept it.

Hopefully all those efforts have yielded enough cash to get you through a temporary financial shortfall. If not, you've got some serious decisions to make. Perhaps it's time for those of you who haven't been able to find a good job to take any job, just to make ends meet. I'd suggest you take a part-time job first so that you'll still have a portion of the day to devote to your search for a good job. If that's still not enough money, it's time to consider selling other, more important assets, such as your jewelry, personal possessions, auto—maybe even your home. Here's when I think you should sit down with your accountant and attorney and consider declaring bankruptcy.

Notice I didn't suggest you contact a bankruptcy lawyer. A professional who specializes in one particular type of action has a tendency, consciously or unconsciously, always to advocate for that action. A surgeon always thinks you need an operation, and a bankruptcy attorney always thinks you should declare bankruptcy. If you do decide to declare bankruptcy, by all means hire a specialist—he or she will help preserve some of your assets—but until then seek out unbiased advice.

There are two basic forms of personal bankruptcy: chapter 7 and chapter 13. In a chapter-7 bankruptcy the court appoints a trustee to sell the debtor's property and distribute the proceeds among the creditors. Depending on the state in which you live, some of your assets may be protected. Florida, for instance, lets you hold on to your home, whatever its value, while New York only lets you keep $10,000 worth of real property. About six months after your assets are sold, you'll receive notification your debts have been discharged—in effect canceled. Chapter-13 bankruptcies, on the other hand, are actually reorganizations. If you have less than $100,000 in unsecured debt and $350,000 in secured debt, the court may be able to bar your creditors from taking any actions while giving you from three to five years to make good. In both chapter 7 and chapter 13 there are some debts—such as child support, alimony, some student loans and taxes, and drunk driving penalties—that will not be erased. In addition chapter 13 does not discharge mortgage debts.

Declaring bankruptcy does have one distinct advantage: It erases most of your debts and lets you get on with your life. But it should only be used as a last resort. While it's not the blot against your soul many fear, it remains a blot against your credit. Declaring bankruptcy can make it difficult to buy or rent homes and autos. And as more and more potential employers use credit reports as a means of prescreening job applicants, a bankruptcy can become a stumbling block to getting a job.

Emergency Finances Checklist

1. Use credit card cash advances to stock food staples.
2. Compile a list of your creditors and how much they're owed.
3. Contact the gas and electric company.
4. Contact the telephone company.
5. Contact your landlord.
6. Contact credit and charge card companies.
7. Contact the bank that holds your home mortgage or equity loan.
8. Contact professionals who are owed money.
9. Go on an austerity budget.
10. Close out IRAs and Keoghs.
11. Go back to the nest and try to borrow money.
12. Ask for inheritances early.
13. Look for and sell dormant assets.
14. Take a part-time job.
15. When all else fails, consider bankruptcy.

Rules for Early Withdrawal of 401K Plan Funds

1. Hardship withdrawals can only be made from the employee's contributions, not from nonelective and matching contributions.
2. Hardship distributions are permitted only if the participant has "an immediate and heavy financial need" and other resources are not "reasonably available" to meet the need.
3. Guidelines for what constitutes "immediate and heavy financial need" are contained in the Internal Revenue Code, but examples include:

   • Medical expenses incurred by the employee, his spouse, or dependents
   • The purchase—excluding mortgage payments—of the employee's principal residence
   • Payment of tuition for the next semester or quarter of postsecondary education for the employee, his spouse, or dependents
   • The need to prevent eviction of the employee from his principal residence or foreclosure on the mortgage on his principal residence

4. According to the Internal Revenue Code, an employer can rely on other resources not being "reasonably available" if the employee represents that the need cannot be relieved

   • Through reimbursement or compensation of insurance
   • By reasonable liquidation of assets

- By cessation of elective contributions or employee contributions
- By other distributions or nontaxable loans from any plans
- By loans from commercial sources

5. Hardship distributions are subject to an additional tax of 10 percent on top of regular income tax.
6. Loans may be made against contributions to 401K plans subject to guidelines in the Internal Revenue Code, but they must be approved by the employer.

Rules for Early Withdrawals from IRA and Keogh (H.R. 10) Accounts

1. Early withdrawals from IRA accounts are subject to a 10 percent penalty tax on top of regular income tax unless

- The individual has died
- The individual has set up a series of roughly equal payments tied to life expectancy (subject to Internal Revenue Codes)
- The individual is mentally or physically disabled and the disability is expected to last longer than a year or lead to death

2. Early withdrawals from Keogh accounts are subject to a 10 percent penalty tax on top of regular income tax unless

- The individual has died
- The individual has set up a series of roughly equal payments tied to life expectancy (subject to Internal Revenue Codes)
- The individual is mentally or physically disabled and the disability is expected to last longer than a year or lead to death
- The withdrawal is to pay otherwise nondeductible catastrophic medical bills (those not in excess of 7.5 percent of your adjusted gross income).

3. Loans may be made against contributions to Keogh plans subject to guidelines in the Internal Revenue Code, but they must be approved by the employer.

CHAPTER 10

Pulling Up Stakes

The blank page, difficult mirror,
gives back only what you were.
—George Seferis

The residential real estate market has always been the best economic indicator of the national psyche. Buying a home is the largest purchase most Americans ever make. Only someone confident about the future feels comfortable committing to a thirty-year home mortgage.

During boom periods, like the 1980s, home prices soar, paralleling rising consumer confidence. With incomes increasing, people decide to take the plunge and buy their first home or move to a larger home. They enter the market in large numbers, strengthening demand, and in turn forcing prices higher. As prices continue to climb, more buyers jump into the market, afraid that waiting will result in their being priced out.

But the reverse is also true. When consumer confidence goes down, as it is now, home prices fall. No longer secure with the economy in general and their jobs in particular, people hesitate to make a thirty-year commitment. Demand drops off; prices stabilize and then begin to fall. As prices tumble, many who would be willing to buy, delay and vacillate instead, waiting for prices to bottom out. All this makes selling a home during a recession very difficult—but not impossible.

Before I take you through the process, however, it's essential to decide whether it's really in your best interest to sell now. Real estate will bounce back. Despite the claims of some newly emerging real estate theorists—who always seem to appear during market slumps—prices will once again start moving upward, probably by the mid-1990s, but at a more natural pace: probably one or two points ahead of inflation. As long as there's a finite amount of land and a growing population, real estate, over the long term, rises in value. By waiting out the recession you may be able to get more money when you sell—and you'll certainly have an easier time of it. That's why I'm advising my clients to hold on to their real estate right now if it's at all possible.

Unfortunately not everyone has that luxury. Whether forced to relocate for job reasons or in order to retire, many people must sell their homes as soon as possible, regardless of the market conditions. If it's simply a matter of needing more space, it makes more sense today to renovate or remodel than to sell and buy something larger. (For information on this option, see chapter 16.) If you must sell, bear in mind that things may not be as bad as they seem. Even though your home may have dropped in value, so has the home you'll be buying. The extent to which you'll actually lose or gain financially depends on the difference between the market conditions of where you currently live and where you intend to move. It's possible to make up in the buy what you lose in the sell and actually come out ahead, or at least break even.

Let's say you're forced to sell your condominium in Boston because your company is transferring you. Three years ago your apartment would have fetched

$250,000, but today it's only worth $225,000. You automatically assume you've lost $25,000, or 10 percent of its value. Actually it depends on where you're being transferred to. If you're going to New York, the apartments you'll be looking at for $225,000 were also previously worth $250,000. Rather than "losing" $25,000, you'll actually break even. If the company transfers you to Houston, you'll end up making money, since apartments priced at $225,000 were selling for $275,000 three years ago. On the other hand, if the company sends you to San Francisco, you'll buy a $225,000 home that was worth the same amount three years earlier, and unfortunately you will have lost $25,000 in the process. Of course this isn't money out of your pocket but rather a decrease in your expected return.

All this discussion of market differences assumes you'll be taking all the proceeds from the sale of your home and using it to buy another. If you're planning on selling your home, buying something less expensive, and using the difference to pay for your living expenses, the market, I'm afraid, has stolen some of your retirement money. You can make up for this, to some extent, by lowering your sights and standards when you turn around and buy. Another option is either to delay retirement and/or to retire but try to stick it out in your current home until the market bounces back.

If you must sell your home in this market, you obviously want to get a good price as quickly as possible. The first secret is getting an accurate assessment of its market value. Despite ups and downs and its apparent emotionality, the real estate market is based in logic. The value of your home is determined not by what you think it's worth, or what buyers think it's worth, but by the selling prices of comparable homes. That's why, while they can help you learn about the market, classified ads aren't a good indication of value. Homes are always priced high to allow room for negotiation and are all too often priced based on the seller's needs and perceptions, not on comparables.

You can find the selling prices of comparable homes in a variety of ways. The sale of a private home or condominium must be recorded by the municipality. This information is compiled by either the county clerk or the registrar of deeds and is open for public inspection. Sales of cooperative apartments aren't recorded by municipalities, since they actually involve the transfer of stock, but may be obtained from a source within the particular building. Getting these numbers is a good starting point, but it's not enough—especially in this market.

In order to get the most accurate assessment of value, you need to pinpoint which of the recently sold homes in your area are the most comparable to yours. Short of a formal appraisal, the best source for this information is a knowledgeable local real estate broker. Go through your local newspaper and determine which three brokers seem to have the most listings in your area. Telephone each and explain you're about to put your home up for sale and would like them to give you a price estimate. There's be no fee for this unless you ask for an appraisal in writing.

If any of the brokers offer judgments over the telephone, discount their number and hang up as soon as possible. A broker can only give a valid estimate after seeing your home and determining how it compares with those properties recently sold in the area. In fact you should press each broker you contact to provide reasons for his or her estimate. The more the broker's number is backed up with details about specific homes in the area, the more accurate it is. For example, one broker might simply say your home is worth $300,000 because she just sold a house around the corner for that price two months ago. Another, more knowledgeable broker, would explain that one home in your area sold for $270,000 four months ago and another sold for $300,000 two months ago. He would note that the $300,000 home had a deck, which yours doesn't, but the $270,000 wasn't kept up as well as yours, so your home falls somewhere in between—probably around $285,000.

Watch out for brokers who are overly optimistic about the value of your home and the possibility of selling quickly. In most cases they're trying to lure you into signing an exclusive listing agreement by playing to your ego and greed. Once they've got you hooked, they'll begin pressuring you to accept a lower price. Your response to brokers' requests for listings is to say, "I'm not prepared to put the house on the market yet, but I'll be back in touch with you when the time comes." If a broker presses you too hard or starts warning of the dire consequences of delay, cut the conversation short and scratch his name off your list. Delay can be costly, but not as damaging as putting a home on the market without adequate preparation. In order to sell your home quickly and profitably in this market, you must assume command of the selling process; it won't be enough just to pass the responsibility on to a broker.

After speaking with brokers you'll find the value of your home isn't a specific dollar amount, but instead falls somewhere within a 20 to 30 percent range. For instance, homes in your area aren't simply worth $200,000; they probably range in price from $185,000 to $215,000. There are several things that determine where within the range your home sells: its specific location in the area; its condition; its features; and the extent to which buyers "fall in love" with it.

Since your aim is to get the most you can for your home as quickly as possible, it makes sense to do everything possible to ensure that it falls in the top end of the range. There's nothing you can do about your home's specific location, and it's foolish to start adding new features now when you're about to sell, since you can't predict buyers' tastes, so you must concentrate on improving its condition and helping it inspire love in buyers.

Take out a pencil and paper and make a thorough, objective inspection of your home. Look for cracks, stains, and other obvious signs of problems. Check all the mechanical aspects of the house: Do doors shut properly? Do fixtures and outlets all work? Are there leaking faucets or toilets that keep flushing? Does every burner on the stove work? Are carpets frayed? Is wallpaper peeling off any walls? Is the grout between bathroom tiles mildewed? Take care of every problem you uncover. If you can spot them, so can buyers.

Then call in an inspector to uncover the problems you can't spot on your own. In this market buyers use anything they can find to try to knock down your price. In order to get top dollar, your home must be in perfect shape. Since they'll be hiring an inspector to go through your home with a fine-tooth comb, why not stage a preemptive strike and pay for your own inspection? This may not keep buyers from having one of their own done, but at least it gives you the chance to take care of potential problems ahead of time. The key is to repair and restore, not to replace. Every dollar you spend repairing will be reflected in your selling price, while dollars spent replacing won't be recouped. For lists of must-do, recommended, and too-expensive projects, consult the chart on page 164.

While you're arranging for repairs, take out a scrub brush and get to work. When your home is put on the market, it should sparkle like a newly cut diamond and be as clean as an operating room. Nothing in its appearance should raise a doubt in a potential buyer. Inside, pay particular attention to your kitchen, bathrooms, and windows. Outside, make sure the front door, walkway, and landscaping are neat and well manicured.

Use this cleaning binge as an opportunity to start thinning out and packing up your possessions. Remove all but this season's clothing from your closets. Clear out your kitchen cabinets, packing away your good dishes and nonessential housewares and appliances. Weed out your furnishings, getting rid of everything that won't be making the move with you. Have a yard sale and get rid of all the junk that's accumulated in your garage, attic, and crawl space. The less you actually have inside your home, the larger and more spacious it appears to a potential buyer. Don't remove all traces of your living there—you'll appear desperate to sell—simply pare down the contents of your home to the minimum.

Now, with your home in tip-top shape, give some thought to its style and decor. While all the personal touches you've added over the years—photos, posters, knickknacks, books—helped turn a house into a home, it's now time to get rid of them and turn it back into a house. In order for buyers to be able to fall in love with a home, it must be in mint condition, spotless, and be a blank page. Your taste may or may not be the same as theirs. By turning your home into a neutral environment you allow them to project their own tastes onto it. The more neutral your home, the more likely it serves as a mirror for buyers, letting them see themselves living there. And once buyers sees themselves standing at your stove or sitting in your living room, they're hooked. So take down the Warhol posters, store away the Victorian bric-a-brac, pack up your collection of Boston Celtic memorabilia, and turn your chocolate-raspberry-swirl home into a plain-vanilla house.

When you've finished repairing, cleaning, thinning out, and depersonalizing your home, it's time to get in touch with your professionals. Another secret to maximizing the proceeds from the sale of your home is to ensure that the transaction moves swiftly. Each day the money isn't in your bank is a day you're losing interest. And the more time buyers must think about what they're doing and worry whether it's the right decision, the more likely they are to get cold feet and walk away.

By contacting your attorney early you can prepare him to be able to write, negotiate, and sign a contract within twenty-four hours of shaking hands. Speaking with your accountant ahead of time allows the two of you to work out and plan for the tax ramifications of the sale and also to determine exactly how flexible you are financially. This financial flexibility is important in a recessionary economy. One way to get top dollar for your home today is to offer to help the buyer with the financing. Rather than knocking down your price you can offer to take back a second mortgage, or perhaps work out some type of rent-with-an-option-to-buy arrangement. Offering flexibility about the financing of the transaction lets you be firmer about the actual price.

Now that your professional team has been given their marching orders, it's time to go back to the brokers you contacted for price estimates. While it's possible to sell your home without a broker, I don't recommend it. You have an emotional stake in your home and therefore aren't in the best position to negotiate its sale. In addition, you want your home to be open for inspection twenty-four hours a day, if need be, not just the hours when you're available. And while you may think not using a broker saves you the traditional 6 percent commission, buyers automatically lower their offers by 6 percent to compensate.

That doesn't mean you shouldn't be cautious about selecting a broker. They're an unusual type of professional. While they're being paid by the seller, they actually spend most of their time with the buyer. And while telling each party they're looking out for their separate interests and representing them, brokers actually represent the deal itself. Let me explain. Brokers are only concerned with closing a deal, any deal. They earn their commission when they bring a buyer and seller together. Brokers are not concerned with getting the seller the best price, or saving the buyer money. All they care about is getting the two parties to agree and then collecting their 6 percent. That's why you should never tell them the minimum you'd be willing to accept—they'll immediately pass this information along to the buyer in order to cinch a deal. As long as you realize that brokers aren't on your side, you can use their ambiguous position to your advantage later on during the negotiations.

Ask your candidate brokers for the names and telephone numbers of their three most recent clients. If a broker refuses, scratch his or her name off your list. Any professional who isn't willing to provide references has something to hide. Contact the recent clients and ask about the broker's sense of urgency and behavior. Find out how many buyers the broker brought around and how long it took to sell the home.

Once you select a broker, he'll ask you to sign what's called either a listing agreement or a brokerage agreement, defining the terms of your relationship. Never sign any such agreement without letting your attorney see it first, and be prepared to negotiate its terms. Generally there are two types of brokerage agreements: exclusive listings and multiple listings.

An exclusive listing gives the broker the exclusive right to sell the property for a stated period of time. Regardless of who actually produces the buyer—even if it's you—the broker is entitled to a commission. This provides him with an incentive to promote and market the property. But at the same time it limits the number of prospective buyers who'll be shown your house, since other brokers, knowing they must share the commission, won't readily bring people by. If you do opt for an exclusive, make sure you receive a written guarantee of how much advertising and promotion will be done in return.

A multiple-listing agreement simply places your home on a master list that is passed among a large number of brokers. It stipulates you'll pay the commission to whichever broker brings in the buyer. This ensures that you'll reach a large audience, since every broker has an equal opportunity to earn the commission. However, in exchange your home won't be promoted heavily since no broker wants to spend money advertising something he or she may not earn the commission from. If you choose to go with a multiple listing, you'll probably need to do your own advertising and promotion, so be prepared to spend some additional dollars. The only thing you might be able to talk the broker into is sponsoring one or two open houses.

Whichever type of agreement you sign, pay careful attention to its fine print. If the contract specifies a selling price, make sure it's at the upper end of the range but not so high it limits your negotiating flexibility. Limit the length of the agreement to two months if at all possible, since you don't want to be stuck with a lousy broker for too long. Make sure the contract details what services the broker provides. Don't accept their verbal assurances—get it in writing. Similarly the contract should note which items in the house, such as appliances and fixtures, are not included in the selling price. Even if you intend to sell these along with the house, hold them in reserve until the negotiation so that you'll have some deal sweeteners available. Try to cut the broker's commission down to 5 percent, if you can, perhaps in exchange for a concession in the length of the agreement. Say, "Okay, I'll sign a ninety-day contract, but in exchange I expect you to cut your commission." Check to see when the contract calls for the commission to be paid. Most agreements, since they're drafted by brokers, state that money is due "when the broker produces a buyer who's ready, willing, and able to buy." Change this so that the money is due "when title actually changes hands." This ensures that you'll only be required to pay the broker after the deal has actually gone through.

With your broker lined up it's time to do some last-minute marketing. Go to every light fixture inside and outside the house and increase the wattage of its bulbs: replace 40-watt bulbs with 60s, 60s with 100s, and spotlights with floodlights. Put the outside lights on a timer so that the house will be bathed in light as soon as the sun sets. Keep your drapes open and shades up at all times, and leave the lights on in any room that's particularly dark so that the home is as light as possible when a buyer enters. Have fresh flowers in various rooms so that there's a pleasant, but not overpowering, scent in the house. If that gets too expensive, try putting some vanilla extract on a light bulb or a stick of cinnamon in a warm oven.

The final element in your marketing plan is a fact sheet about your home. Buyers often see five or six houses every day. They have a hard time remembering each one. By providing them a handout you make sure your home stands out from the crowd. This handout can be as simple or as complex as budgets allow: For a $100,000, one-bedroom apartment it might be a single 8-½-by-11-inch page, while a $500,000, six-bedroom home sitting on two and a half acres might merit an eight-page illustrated brochure. However extensive it is, your handout should itemize and describe all the features of the home, provide floor plans and dimensions of each room, and note the offering price, total square footage, monthly maintenance and utility costs, and approximate taxes. In addition the handout should include important information about the building and/or neighborhood. For example, mention the accessibility to public transportation and shopping and the quality of the school district if they reflect positively on the property. There's a sample handout on pages 165 to 166.

Next place a pile of the handouts by the front door, hand a key to the broker, and get out of the way. I believe your presence can only hurt your chances of making a deal. Think about what your reactions would be if you came to look at a home and the current residents were present. Would you be comfortable opening closets or cabinets? How freely would you voice your criticisms to the broker? Remember, you want to create a blank page on which the buyers can project their own dreams. Your presence keeps them from visualizing themselves in the house. Give your broker a cutoff time for showing the house—9:00 P.M., for example—and tell them you want at least fifteen minutes' warning before they bring anyone by. Up until the cutoff time be prepared to vacate the premises, along with your kids and pets, on short notice. It may be a bit of a nuisance, but it's a cross you must bear if you want to sell profitably and quickly during a recession.

If you do everything I've suggested so far, it

shouldn't take too long for the broker to telephone you with news you've got an offer. However, if you find no offers are forthcoming after three weeks have passed, remove the house from the market. After around a month real estate listings go stale. Brokers consciously or unconsciously believe there's something wrong with the property and stop bringing buyers to see it. You should also avoid knocking your price down while the house is being shown—that's yet another indication of desperation and leads buyers and brokers to feel they can talk you down dramatically. Instead pull back for a month and rethink your pricing. If you've been misled by brokers who overestimated your home's value, lower your asking price accordingly and start the process all over again.

When you do receive an offer, it's important to remain calm—you're about to enter into a delicate *pas de deux*. Your response to the first offer is very important. Generally it indicates to both the buyer and the broker what you'll be willing to accept and sets the tone for the whole negotiation. Let's say your home is listed at $200,000 and you receive an offer of $180,000. If you respond with a counteroffer of $190,000, you're indicating to the buyer and broker you're willing to split the difference between their initial offer and your counteroffer. In other words, you'd accept $185,000. A better response would be to make a counteroffer to the broker of $198,000 and indicate to the broker that you're willing to negotiate, but the initial offer is too low.

It makes good sense to use the broker as the intermediary for the negotiations. First, it keeps emotions out of the process. If you don't like the buyer or the buyer doesn't like you, that may affect your judgment. The personalities of the parties should have nothing to do with whether or not a deal is made. You should be willing to sell your home to Attila the Hun, who plans on tearing it down and turning it into a garbage dump, as long as you get your price. Second, the broker's natural desire to make a deal can become a tool for convincing the buyers to increase their offer. If you appear resolute in your negotiations, the broker works on the buyer instead. And every message you want sent to the buyer will be amplified by the now-eager broker.

If the buyer responds to your slight price reduction with a more favorable offer, respond in kind. You aren't looking to make a killing here, or to win. What counts is that both parties find common ground and come away satisfied. Let's say the buyer responds to your counter offer of $198,000 with an offer of $190,000. You can then indicate to the broker your willingness to meet at $195,000.

If, on the other hand, the buyer starts playing games, signal your annoyance. Perhaps the buyer comes back with a small increase mirroring your own decrease, say an offer of $182,000. Don't respond with another price reduction—that would indicate your willingness to haggle bit by bit until you reach the midpoint. Instead tell the broker that while you're willing to listen to reasonable offers and negotiate, this buyer doesn't appear to understand you've made a conscientious effort to price your home properly. Say that unless they're willing to be realistic, you're not interested in any further negotiations with them. Hopefully this instills enough fear in the broker that she'll pressure the buyer to stop playing games. If the buyer doesn't respond, he probably wasn't seriously interested anyway, so you're better off breaking off the process as early as possible.

Many times after you've made a counteroffer, the broker comes back to you with a plea from the buyer. "They really love this home," the broker says, "but they just can't afford to spend any more than

$190,000." That's an opening for you to suggest a second mortgage or some other alternative financing arrangement. If you still find yourselves apart by a few thousand dollars, call in the broker, and say, "I think we're stuck here. I'd really like to sell to these people, but I need $195,000, and they can't come up with any more than $193,000. What would you suggest we do?" This is a subtle invitation to the broker to lower her commission. Faced with the choice of making $2,000 less or nothing at all, brokers invariably opt to make up the difference.

Remain flexible throughout the negotiations. By all means stick to your guns—but be sensible and remember that during a recession it's better to have $200,000 in cash than $210,000 in principle. You can't use the principle to pay for your own new home or to support yourself during retirement.

Preselling Fix-up Project Checklist

Must Dos

1. Clean entire home thoroughly
2. Clean tile grout
3. Eliminate or conceal odors
4. Exterminate completely
5. Increase bulb wattage
6. Repair appliances
7. Repair existing wallpaper
8. Repair fixtures
9. Repair water damage
10. Replace broken windows
11. Replace shower curtain
12. Thin out closets and furnishings

Recommended Projects

1. Add strategic mirrors
2. Have home preinspected and repair potential "deal breakers"
3. Refinish cabinets
4. Refinish countertops
5. Refinish porcelain fixtures
6. Repaint walls and ceilings

Too Expensive

1. Hang new wallpaper
2. Lay new flooring
3. Replace appliances and/or cabinets
4. Replace countertops
5. Replace fixtures
6. Regrout tiles

Sample Home Handout

27 East Elm Street
Cooperative Apartment #2
A Landmark Building

Features: A 1,700 square-foot, seven-room duplex apartment in a turn-of-the-century limestone mansion located a few steps away from Pine Avenue. The apartment was extensively renovated in 1989 and was featured in the *New City Gazette* on February 7, 1990.

Price: $750,000
Maintenance: $1,260 per month
Tax deductibility: 40 percent

First Floor: 12-foot ceilings; entry foyer with closet; powder room; fully enclosed spiral staircase with trompe l'oeil mural and hand-painted finishes

Living Room: 22 × 22; gilt trim; oak paneling; stenciled ceiling
Conservatory: 7 × 12; black-and-white marble floor; muraled ceiling
Eat-in Kitchen: 10 × 15; tile countertops and backsplash; unique hand-painted wooden floor; restaurant range; stacked washer and dryer; custom refrigerator/freezer

Second Floor:

Master Bedroom: 27 × 16; three closets; antique marble wood-burning fireplace; glazed fabric wall coverings
Master Bedroom: teak paneling; teak floor; spacious storage lofts
Second Bedroom: 10 × 15; muraled ceiling; casement windows opening on three exposures; imported carpeting
Second Bathroom: rose-marble floor and shower

Floor Plan: attached

Building Information: elevator equipped; keyed security systems; oil heat, 24-hour doorman; full-time, on-premises superintendent.

Building Mortgage: $367,000 due in 1997 at 10.5 percent interest
Stockholders Equity: $899,826
Maintenance History: 1989—$1,186; 1990—$1,186; 1991—$1,260

Immediate Area: upper-income residential neighborhood; within walking distance of supermarket, dry cleaner, drugstore, public elementary and middle schools, bus stop; Roman Catholic church, and reform synagogue; part of award-winning central high school district; Lutheran and Methodist churches within 5-minute drive

Note: The information contained herein is believed to be accurate but isn't guaranteed.

PART III

GOING ON THE OFFENSIVE

Carpe diem,
quam minimum credula postero!
(Seize the day,
put no trust in the morrow!)
—Horace

CHAPTER 11

Getting Reemployed Quickly

Does the road wind uphill all the way?
Yes, to the very end.
Will the day's journey take the whole long day?
From morn to night, my friend.
—Christina Georgina Rossetti

Finding a job during a recession isn't impossible. Even as some companies lay off workers, new businesses start up and expand. According to most reliable statistics, more jobs will be created than eliminated in the coming year. That means there are increasing numbers of jobs available. But that's little solace if you've been unemployed for any length of time.

Today's job market is extremely crowded. Employers have more choices than ever before. Three years ago it was tough for an employer to find five qualified candidates for a position—and every one of those individuals were being actively recruited by the competition as well. Today an employer can choose from among fifty qualified candidates. And it's the candidates who are feeling competitive pressures. Three years ago a white-collar worker could count on getting a new, better-paying job in from one to three months. Today it's taking from five to eight months. And rather than paying more, the new position is, at best, on the same salary level.

The secret of speeding up this job search is to sell yourself like a commodity. If your job was selling widgets, what would be the first thing you'd do? You'd pick a widget and take a look at it, figuring out what makes it a good product, what are its benefits and features. Then you'd decide how best to communicate those benefits and features to widget buyers. That's the same process you must go through in developing a job campaign. You are the widget. Remarkably few people approach job hunting in this manner. Instead they fall back on the inefficient job search techniques they learned years ago. Returning to the employment market after being laid off is like rejoining the singles scene after being widowed or divorced. To be successful, you must understand the new environment and update your repertoire accordingly. The first renovation project should be your résumé.

Even in this electronic information age, a one- or two-page, black-and-white, typed or printed career history is still required by every potential employer. Despite the puffery and exaggeration that have become commonplace, most résumés are actually designed to help the employer, not the employee. The traditional chronological listing of where you've worked and for how long is a negative screening device. Potential employers want to scan through résumés quickly—hence their repeated demands that they be kept short—and find something to disqualify the candidate.

What do they look for? Lack of experience and expertise first, to weed out the unqualified. But they also put résumés through a more subjective analysis. Some personnel executives admit they eliminate candidates from schools or companies they don't like. The rationalization is that those corporate philosophies and academic styles won't fit in with their organization. They may also discard résumés of candidates who have worked for one company for too long a period of time, or who have jumped from one company to another too often. The résumé reader's goal is to cut the number of potential candidates to a manageable size.

Therefore your goal should be to prepare a résumé that minimizes potential negatives and maximizes positive achievements, thus improving the chances of getting through the initial screening process and being invited for an interview. That's the sole purpose of a résumé: to get your foot in the door. It's the interview that actually lands you the job.

Since most potentially negative factors come from your career chronology, it's wise to stress personal attributes rather than individual jobs. It's easy to come up with a long list of positive qualities and skills: honest, experienced, reliable, hardworking. . . . But remember, we're in a recession in which average employees are getting laid off. Employers today are looking for exceptional people. Having the characteristics of an Eagle Scout just isn't enough anymore. Today you must be a profit center. Rather than being the employee who's honest and who helps little old ladies across the street, you must be the employee who develops a plan to reduce theft and who provides a profitable escort service for little old ladies. Simply put, exceptional employees are those who make the company more money, either by cutting costs or by boosting revenues.

Instead of describing yourself to an employer in all-American, apple-pie clichés, you need to detail your achievements; and these should be translated into dollars and cents. Using your old résumé as a reference, retrace your career looking for instances when your efforts and leadership resulted in cost savings or revenue increases. Make sure to include specific data, such as percentages, dollar amounts, or lengths of time. Don't simply say you reorganized the production department—explain how, with 20 percent less staff, you were able to double output. Rather than stating that your design won an award, stress that it was developed in half the time, at one-third the cost, and resulted in a 15 percent boost in sales. If you can't come up with exact numbers, use estimates—as long as claims don't appear to be outrageous or manufactured out of thin air, they'll be accepted as true.

Even though you'll begin your résumé with a list of career accomplishments, including a career chronology is unavoidable—employers and personnel executives have every right to know where you've worked and for how long. But by downplaying the time line you can force them to focus on what sets you apart positively rather than negatively.

An achievement-oriented résumé also fits a wider variety of jobs than a strictly chronological one. When looking at a chronological résumé, the reader automatically infers a typical step-by-step progression up the ladder in a particular industry or career. Unless the position they have open and the next logical step in your career match identically, your résumé is discarded. Stressing actual accomplishments takes you out of a pedestrian climb up one particular ladder and forces the reader to think.

It's possible to minimize potential stumbling blocks by correctly formating your career chronology. For example, if you've had a history of quickly hopping from one job to another, include salary figures and job descriptions that show that each move was made for good reasons. If, on the other hand, you've remained with one company for a long period of time, demonstrate a progression within the company. Treat each promotion, change in responsibilities, and salary increase as a separate entry in your chronology, demonstrating you haven't just been treading water. Gaps in a chronology can be eliminated by detailing how the time was used—to write a book or go back to school, for example. There's a sample résumé on pages 184 to 185.

I'm not advocating turning your résumé into a work of fiction. While there's nothing wrong with "coloring" reality, outright lying comes back to haunt you. Lies may help you get an interview, or maybe even land a job, but more time and energy will be devoted to covering your tracks than to doing a good job. And even if you do manage to thrive while camouflaging your past, if the truth ever emerges—and it invariably does—you're dead.

Even though the content of your résumé is somewhat unorthodox, its appearance should be traditional. Unusual typefaces, colored paper, photographs, videotapes, and other gimmicks are indications of a lack of respect for business norms, not a sign of creativity. Stick to 10- or 12-point serif typefaces printed in black ink on white paper; and try to contain the information within two pages.

After completing a new résumé your next step is figuring out what to do with it. Once again, it's vital to steer clear of the standard approach. Typically job hunters pick up copies of local newspapers, professional journals, and trade magazines, circle all the help-wanted advertisements they're even remotely interested in, and blindly send out résumés in response. When there are few openings, traditional job hunters do a bulk mailing to all potential employers. If those approaches fail to generate leads, they then turn to an employment agency for help. In the best of times these techniques are inefficient; during a recession they're useless.

Relying on help-wanted advertisements and bulk mailings to find a job during a recession is like depending on lottery winnings to finance retirement. It could work out, but the odds are infinitesimal. Remember, there are literally hundreds of others applying for the same positions and soliciting the same companies. Unless you're perfect for the job, your résumé ends up in the circular file. By all means answer ads that seem right for you—but don't stretch it in the mistaken notion that volume increases your chances. All it does is increase the number of rejections you must deal with. That's what happened to me.

After the bank chose not to pick up my contract, I had to look for work. I answered hundreds of ads for jobs—a few I was truly interested in, but most were desperate stretches. After repeated rejections I came up with the brilliant idea of doing a bulk mailing. Thinking myself creative and innovative, I decided to send a letter and résumé to every company in the Fortune 500 that had dropped in rank that year. In each letter I indicated my willingness to help reverse their declining fortunes. I got four responses: One was a form rejection and the other three were notes from personnel people scolding me for presumptuousness.

In my opinion head hunters aren't much help either. Most earn their money from companies looking to fill positions. They do not represent job seekers. The head hunter receives a commission when they find an acceptable candidate for the client. Since it's easier to seek out individuals who are employed by competitors of the client company and convince them to shift allegiances, that's where they concentrate their efforts. You're more likely to hear from a head hunter about a job opening when you're employed and not looking than when you're unemployed and desperate.

So how should you market yourself? By networking. Recent studies indicate that almost 70 percent of jobs are filled through personal contacts of some kind. The reason networking is so widespread and successful is that it benefits all parties. The intermediary makes a judgment on whether the two parties are mutually acceptable, greatly increasing the odds that any scheduled meeting will be successful. If I know you're looking for a job selling widgets for a relaxed sales organization, and I also know my friend at Acme Widgets, who runs an easygoing shop, is looking for an experienced widget seller, the odds are good you'd be right for each other. Acme Widgets benefits by getting a qualified candidate. The job seeker benefits by being directed to an interested potential employer. And the intermediary earns points from both employer and employee.

Rather than sending out résumés indiscriminately, the best way to find a job, especially during a recession when the job market is crowded with candidates, is to get advice and guidance from everyone you know. Telephone personal and business contacts and tell them you're looking for a new job. Explain what type of job and employer you're looking for. Don't hesitate to tout your accomplishments: Even those who know you well may not be fully aware of all your skills and abilities. Stress that rather than just seeking a job, you're also looking for guidance and advice. Express your willingness to meet with individuals simply to discuss opportunities in different industries.

People are naturally hesitant to meet with job seekers, whether or not they have openings. But everyone loves being treated as an expert. By opening yourself up to exploratory meetings you're in effect renting others' Rolodexes. I may only be able to direct you to

one person in the widget industry who doesn't have
any openings right now. But by meeting with my pal
at Acme Widgets and asking for his help and advice
you expand the network enormously. He in turn can
put you in touch with other widget people, one of
whom may have an opening or be aware of a position
elsewhere.

Don't feel as though you're inconveniencing people
or overstepping bounds. The business world works on
contacts and favors. If I help you, somewhere down the
road you'll be willing to help me. Similarly if a friend
of mine helps you, they know I'll be willing to help a
friend of theirs. And so on and so on. Working your
way into this interconnected quid pro quo network of
business is the real secret to lining up job interviews.

Earlier this year I opened up my Rolodex to a client's wife. She was looking to return to the job market
after having been a full-time mother for five years. Un-
sure about what type of career to pursue, she needed
advice and guidance. I put her in touch with business
aquaintances in four different fields. She met with
each, and by the time she left their offices, she had another sixteen names. She scheduled meetings with
these contacts, which resulted in a couple of job offers,
but more importantly a whole new set of contacts. By
the time she landed a job, she had an enviable network
of her own.

Once an interview is lined up, however, you've
only yourself to rely on. No matter how impressive
your résumé or how highly recommended you're recommended, the final hiring decision depends on coming across well in an interview. And the best way to do
that is to be prepared. This preparation involves more
than just wearing a clean shirt or blouse and popping
a breath mint. It means learning everything you possi-

bly can about the company in general, and the interviewer in particular.

If the interview came as the result of networking, telephone the intermediary and ask about the person you'll be meeting and the company he or she works for. Next go to the library and research the company and its place within its industry. Consult newspapers, magazines, and trade journals. Read between the lines in an effort to identify the character or personality of the company. Is the staff made up of identical button-down clones or easygoing "intrapreneurs"? If it's a public company, try to get its three most recent annual reports. Read the letters from the chairman and president with an eye toward determining the corporate philosophy. Study the 10K or 10Q report for a generally objective view of the company's finances.

You may never actually get a chance to reveal all your knowledge during the interview, but don't feel as though it's a wasted effort. The more knowledge you have, the more comfortable you'll be and the better you'll come across. I once had to negotiate a very complex and delicate real estate transaction with a high-powered corporate executive. During the week prior to the meeting I dug up all the information I could about him. I found out he had been married to the same woman for thirty years and had two grown children. I discovered he was a graduate of West Point and had served ten years in the military. His hobbies, I learned, were reading about the Civil War and restoring antique automobiles. Throughout my week-long negotiation with him I don't think I used the information more than once. Yet it was extremely valuable. From the moment I walked into his office, I was totally at ease. I felt as if I had known him for years. My confidence and comfort in turn relaxed him. It was one of the easiest and most successful negotiations I've ever done.

During your preparations think about how you'll answer specific questions as well as what questions you should ask. For a look at commonly asked questions, and good questions to ask, see the lists on pages 186 and 187. Don't memorize set answers to all these questions. You want to come across as polished and professional, not stiff and robotic. Just outline concise answers that stress your positive traits, abilities, and experience. If you have any deficiencies that may come up in conversation, be prepared to address them.

Keep right on doing research up until the morning of the interview. Before you leave for the meeting, read the newspaper. The interviewer may bring up a story in the news and ask how you think it affects the industry. Daily newspaper reading is a particular indicator of mine. Whenever I interview someone, I try to determine if he or she has read the morning paper. To me you can't be a fully functional business person unless you know what's happening in the world.

Interview preparation is physical as well as mental. Most interviewers make a judgment of a job candidate within the first three minutes of the meeting and then spend the rest of the conversation looking for evidence to back up their initial judgment. Interview clothing should be conservative and businesslike. Don't worry about being overdressed. Even if everyone else in the company is wearing blue jeans, your being dressed in a suit indicates how seriously you take yourself, the job, and the interview process. Men should wear a conservative shirt, suit, and tie; women a tasteful suit or a skirt and blouse. Of course clothing should be clean and pressed and shoes should be polished. Refrain from making personal style statements. Avoid loud ties, unusual colors, or anything that smacks of sexuality. Jewelry should be kept to a minimum: men should wear only a watch and a wedding ring; women should opt for a single simple bracelet or necklace and stud earrings. Grooming is as important as clothing. Getting a haircut and/or manicure the day before an interview might be a good idea. Certainly get a good night's sleep so that you don't look tired or sickly. Pop a breath mint prior to the interview, but be sure to spit it out before you enter the building.

Poor manners can be the kiss of death in an interview. As soon as you enter the interviewer's office, make eye contact, walk directly toward her, and extend your hand. Maintaining eye contact, introduce yourself using her name as well as your own, smile, and shake her hand firmly. Thank her for taking the time to meet with you. Remain standing until the interviewer invites you to sit down.

Take your lead from the interviewer. If offered a snack or a cup of coffee, accept only if the interviewer has already indicated she'll be having something as well. Rather than simply asking, "Would you like a cup of coffee," good interviewers will take the pressure off you by asking, "Would you like to join me in a cup of coffee." Don't smoke even if she does, and don't remove your suit jacket unless she suggests it.

You can learn a great deal about how the interview will be conducted by the way the interviewer sets the stage. When an interviewer keeps his suit jacket on and remains behind a desk, motioning you to take a seat in front of him, expect an interrogation. If the interviewer has his jacket off, motions for you to sit down, and then comes from behind the desk to join you, expect a conversation.

Whether you're about to be cross-examined or have a chat, pay attention to your body language. Sit up straight with your back against the back of the chair. Never cross your arms across your chest—it's a sign of antagonism. Instead keep your hands folded in your lap, occasionally lifting them by placing your elbows rather than forearms on the arms of the chair. Make sure your gestures are subtle and smooth rather than jerky and dramatic. Lean forward to indicate your interest in what the interviewer is saying, then lean back again to demonstrate thoughtfulness. Keep both feet flat on the floor directly in front of the chair, occasionally crossing your legs at the ankle if you become uncomfortable. Maintain eye contact, but don't get into a staring match. Never, ever look at your watch or stare out the window—it's a sign you're bored.

Try to initiate the conversation with a light comment about something interesting in the office or, if you must, the weather. Starting in a friendly manner indicates your eagerness to have a civil conversation. After all, both parties have the same goal—discovering if your needs and the company's mesh. Let the interviewer do most of the talking and control the flow of conversation, but feel free to ask relevant questions. While abilities and expertise can be assumed from the contents of a résumé, interpersonal skills can only be demonstrated in an interview. Your goal is to convey your courtesy, energy, and enthusiasm; to show the interviewer you can get along with others. If you were the top candidate for the job, this may be all that's needed to get the position.

When the interviewer asks questions, don't feel as though you must rush to answer. Give yourself a moment to collect your thoughts and present a cogent response. Generally interview questions don't have right and wrong answers. They're an attempt by the interviewer to learn how you organize thoughts and present feelings, ideas, and opinions. Draw on your research and preparation for answers, but don't feel as though there's a script etched in stone. The more comfortable you are with the interviewer, and the more relaxed your responses, the better you'll come across.

Many interviewers throw at least one negative question at every candidate. It's usually a general query along the lines of "What would you say are your weaknesses?" This isn't an attempt to discover some hidden problem you may have. It's simply a way for the interviewer to gauge the strength of your ego. The best way to respond to such a general negative question is to talk about a part of your personality or life that has nothing to do with job performance. For example, tell the questioner you've never had the chance to read the complete works of Shakespeare, so you've decided to take a class at the local college. The trick is to select and describe an innocuous weakness, and then indicate that you're taking steps to correct it.

Answering specific negative questions is tougher. Remember, the person on the other side of the desk has had a chance to study your résumé in detail. If there's anything missing, she'll be sure to spot it and perhaps bring it up. If asked why you were fired from a job, say you were asked to do something illegal, immoral, or unethical. If unexplained gaps in your résumé are brought up, blame them on a family emergency, which needed your undivided attention. When an interviewer points out your lack of experience in some area, agree and explain what measures you're taking to correct the deficiency. Whenever you're asked a specific negative question, give a logical response that the interviewer can neither verify nor pursue—and then hope she drops the matter.

Be careful of seemingly innocent, open-ended questions, such as "Tell me all about yourself." While it's possible to hit these lob pitches for tape-measure home runs, it's just as easy to swing and miss by saying something foolish or inappropriate. Rather than using this as an opportunity to regale the questioner with your life story, briefly state your accomplishments and stress your ability and eagerness to do the job. If she presses you for more information, ask her to be more specific. It's particularly important for older job applicants to refrain from blowing their own horns too loudly or too long. In many cases an older applicant has more experience than an interviewer, and overselling can turn you into a potential threat.

That happened to me once. I applied for a job with a real estate investment company and was interviewed by two men approximately ten years younger than myself. The meeting went swimmingly until one of the interviewers asked me what I would do if I was in their position. Letting my ego get the better of me, I began to reel off a comprehensive strategy to develop the company's portfolio. When I began, they were both very interested, even excited with what I had to say. But the more I explained, the more they realized I would be a threat to them. In the course of five minutes their expressions went from interest to excitement to fear. Needless to say, I didn't get the job.

Beware of interviewers who try to maneuver you into stating your salary requirements. In all monetary negotiations the side that first mentions a price goes on the defensive. If the job candidate suggests a salary, it allows the interviewer to begin negotiating the number down. On the other hand, when the interviewer is the first to mention a number, the candidate has the opportunity to negotiate it higher. Do your best to deflect all appeals to lay your cards on the table first. Try turning the question around. Say, "I'm sure you have a good idea of the market value of people with my skills and experience." Then ask, "What does this company normally pay people like me?" If the interviewer continues to press, explain you're concerned with a total package including benefits and career opportunities, not just salary.

The interviewer signals that his questions are exhausted by asking if you have any questions for him. If you have any unanswered questions, feel free to ask them. If all your questions have been answered, ask instead for an estimate of how long it will be before a decision is reached. The interviewer indicates the meeting is over by standing and thanking you for coming in to see him. At this point, stand up, thank him—by name—for the opportunity to be interviewed, restate your interest in the position, shake his hand firmly, say you look forward to hearing from him, and leave.

When you get back home, immediately write a thank-you letter to the interviewer summarizing how your needs and the company's seem to match and again stressing your interest in the position. Follow up with a second, similar note if you don't hear from the interviewer after three weeks.

If the interviewer responds negatively, either in writing or over the telephone, don't get angry or depressed. You have a rare opportunity to get some firsthand advice. Write the interviewer and ask for his help. Explain that you're interested in polishing your interview skills and are hoping he could point out any weaknesses in your presentation. Thank him profusely in advance. If nothing else, you'll get a good critique. You may even be able to add him to your network. Who knows? He could even provide the lead that results in your landing a job.

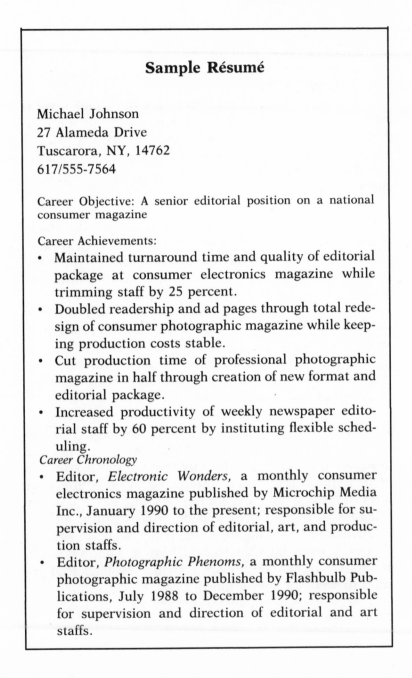

Sample Résumé

Michael Johnson
27 Alameda Drive
Tuscarora, NY, 14762
617/555-7564

Career Objective: A senior editorial position on a national consumer magazine

Career Achievements:
- Maintained turnaround time and quality of editorial package at consumer electronics magazine while trimming staff by 25 percent.
- Doubled readership and ad pages through total redesign of consumer photographic magazine while keeping production costs stable.
- Cut production time of professional photographic magazine in half through creation of new format and editorial package.
- Increased productivity of weekly newspaper editorial staff by 60 percent by instituting flexible scheduling.

Career Chronology
- Editor, *Electronic Wonders,* a monthly consumer electronics magazine published by Microchip Media Inc., January 1990 to the present; responsible for supervision and direction of editorial, art, and production staffs.
- Editor, *Photographic Phenoms,* a monthly consumer photographic magazine published by Flashbulb Publications, July 1988 to December 1990; responsible for supervision and direction of editorial and art staffs.

- Completed course work for MBA degree, September 1987 to June 1988.
- Managing Editor, *Photo Retailing,* a biweekly photographic trade magazine published by Photo Retailing Publishing Corp., January 1987 to August 1987; responsible for design and supervision of copy flow and page production systems.
- News Editor, *Seneca Eagle,* a weekly newspaper published by Seneca Eagle Press, August 1983 to December 1986; responsible for management and supervision of full- and part-time reporting staff of 15.

Education

- Bachelor of Arts in American Literature from the State University of New York at Seneca
- Master of Business Administration from the State University of New York at Unadilla

The Ten Most Commonly Asked Interview Questions

1. Why do you want to work here?
2. What makes you think you're qualified for this job?
3. Why did you leave your last job?
4. What are your strengths and weaknesses?
5. What are your career and personal goals?
6. Where do you see yourself in five years?
7. What did you like and dislike about previous jobs?
8. How would you characterize your work and management styles?
9. Have you ever had to deal with a difficult boss or subordinate?
10. What are your greatest personal and professional accomplishments?

Ten Good Questions to Ask an Interviewer

1. What are the major responsibilities of this position?
2. What would you consider the major challenges facing this position?
3. Whom does the person in this position report to?
4. How much staff support will be available?
5. Has the budget for this department been increasing or decreasing?
6. What's the work atmosphere like in this company?
7. What happened to the person who previously held the position?
8. What would you consider the drawbacks to the position?
9. What opportunities for advancement are there in the company?
10. Where do you see the company headed in the next five years?

CHAPTER 12

Buying the Home of Your Dreams

Festina lente.
(Make haste slowly.)
—Suetonius

Recessions are almost universally viewed as dismal periods in our lives. And for the past eleven chapters I've done little to change this perception. Back in chapter 1, I explained that recessions bring opportunities as well as problems. But all my advice about protecting your stream of income and savings, and what to do if the defenses don't work, has probably brought your spirits back down to where they were before picking up this book. Well, I'm going to try to resurrect your optimism: There has never been a better time to buy a home; and there's never been a time when you get so much home for so little money.

Residential real estate has hit rock bottom. According to the National Association of Home Builders, housing starts in 1991 will drop to about 1.1 million, the lowest mark since 1982. As I write these words, banks are lowering the interest rates they charge borrowers. I believe that once the prime lending rate drops below 9 percent, home prices will stabilize and sales will pick up in those areas where the housing recession occurred first. The problem with residential real estate hasn't been a lack of qualified buyers—the money is available and people are as anxious to buy a home as ever. What happened was they were frightened out of the market.

Real estate prices became inflated in the early to mid 1980s. By soaring to record heights they led many people to believe that real estate had literally become a short-term investment. This widespread notion led to further price inflation as buyers leaped into the market in order to catch the comet's tail. But when prices grew beyond the reach of most consumers, the high-flying market reached its apex and started heading back down to earth. Under the normal laws of capitalism, sellers, seeing the demand fall off, would have lowered their prices in response. But the 1980s operated under an entirely different set of laws.

Owners who hadn't yet sold homes, and developers who weren't finished building and selling projects, refused to admit that prices had gotten too high and had to come down. Private sellers had already mentally added the inflated value of the property to their mental bank books. Some counted on being able to finance their retirements with this money. Developers were in worse shape. They actually borrowed money based on the inflated value, and now had to pay it back. Whether through greed or desperation, neither group of sellers lowered their prices.

With buyers not being able to afford to buy, and sellers not lowering their prices, the market stagnated. Sales slowed to a crawl. Yet the pressures to sell remained constant. People still retired, lost jobs, got transferred, had babies, or became widowed. Finally the logic of capitalism asserted itself, as it always does, and sellers relented. Prices started coming down. But still the market remained dead in the water.

In an interesting turnabout, it was the buyers now who were responsible for the lull. Once prices started dropping, they hesitated. If prices had dropped 10 percent, they asked themselves, why not wait until they drop 20 percent? As prices continued to fall, buyers feared buying too soon. Unlike sellers, they aren't under pressure—the decision to buy a home is entirely self-generated. But as soon as mortgage rates fall below 9 percent, I believe the vast majority of buyers will realize they should strike while the iron is hot. They'll pressure themselves to take advantage of the economic situation.

This pressure will lead to an increase in demand, which will start the pendulum swinging in the other direction. As soon as the surplus of homes that have sat on the market for the past three years dries up, prices will begin to climb again. The National Association of Realtors is forecasting that sales of new home and existing homes will bottom out this year and begin to rebound in 1992. That means right now, when mortgage rates have been lowered to stimulate the economy, and while there's still a surplus of homes up for sale, is the absolute perfect time to buy. And if you're willing to sacrifice a bit, and work at buying, you'll be able to buy a better home than you ever dreamed possible.

Forget about any lingering fears you may harbor. Sure it's a big financial obligation. But owning a home is still the single best financial move anyone can make. And once you learn to look on a mortgage as a monthly bill, not a gigantic thirty-year ball and chain, the numbers become less daunting. In the final analysis, whether you're single or married, are childless or have children, the advantages of home ownership far outweigh the disadvantages.

The pundits who have been proclaiming that the

home is no longer the foundation of our financial lives are dead wrong. Regardless of the recent real estate malaise, over the long haul the value of a home increases at a greater rate than inflation. If you choose wisely and buy a home for $200,000 today, in five years it will be worth $240,000. And consider this: Your $40,000 down payment on a $200,000 house grows in value as if it really was $200,000. Over the thirty years of the loan the dollars used to pay it back are constantly shrinking in value. In addition, this is an investment you retain control over. You can't influence the decisions of the companies whose stock you hold, but you can make sure your home is well maintained.

The equity you build up in a home can serve as the collateral for other important financial moves, including launching a business, renovating the home itself, buying a second home, or buying undeveloped land. It can even serve as the source of money for a child's college tuition or your own retirement. As if all those advantages weren't enough, home ownership is also America's best tax shelter. Not only is a large portion of monthly mortgage payments deductible, but the profit made when the home is sold can be either deferred or eliminated entirely, depending on the age of the seller and what's done with the money.

Even with all these financial benefits, I tell my clients the primary reasons to buy a home are actually emotional. Once ensconced in a home, you'll feel more secure and satisfied. Home ownership speeds the maturation process. A new sense of confidence will be carried over into your career. And sharing the struggles and joys of ownership can bring a couple or family even closer together.

The first step in this magical journey is calculating how much you can afford to spend on a home. Begin by discounting everything you've ever heard from real

estate brokers, bankers, or parents about home affordability. All these self-proclaimed experts have built-in
biases. Brokers are solely concerned with closing deals
as quickly as possible, and rely on a simple formula of
doubling yearly income. This has nothing to do with
what you can actually afford to spend on shelter. A
banker's only interested in making sure the loan is
paid back. Therefore they systematically decrease affordability by taking a percentage of monthly income—generally between 28 and 30—and stating
that's what you can afford to spend on shelter each
month. Parents are, consciously or unconsciously, concerned that their children don't get wiped out and return to the nest. Trust me—I have four children. Until
it comes time for them to sell their own home, they
don't believe anyone should spend more than one
week's salary on shelter.

Once your head is cleared of these inaccurate rules
of thumb, take a ride to the local bookstore and pick
up a mortgage book. When you return home, take out
a pencil and paper, a calculator, and your checkbook.
Or if you prefer, you can use the chart on page 199.
Write down what you're currently spending on shelter
each month. If you still live at home, or your rent is
absurdly low, estimate what you would normally be
paying.

Next start listing expenses you'd be willing to cut
or eliminate in exchange for owning a home. I know
that you cut back on your life-style while coming up
with a six-month cash reserve back in chapter 5, but
you've got to try to cut back even more. In years past
I advised clients to stretch affordability by assuming
that income would increase between 5 and 10 percent
each year. In all good conscience I can't say advise this
anymore. At best, during this recession your income
may keep pace with inflation. In most cases, however,

it won't. But since this is the opportunity of a lifetime, you've got to stretch as far as possible. Remember, you're no longer buying a home for just a few short years, then counting on selling it and buying another. Today home buyers must look for a home in which they'll be comfortable for ten or more years. I know you can't get water from a stone, but in a recession home buyers must squeeze every pebble they can find. Add the amount you can save to your current rent. The total is your maximum rent.

I used the term *rent*, not *mortgage payment* for a good reason. This total doesn't reflect the tax deductibility of mortgage payments. To determine your maximum mortgage payment, multiply your maximum rent by your marginal tax bracket and add the result to the rent figure. Let me explain how this works. Assume you live in New York City and after going through the previous steps come up with a maximum rent number of $1,000. On the $1,000 you would be paying federal, state, and local taxes adding up to about 42 percent. When the $1,000 becomes a mortgage payment, the taxes vanish. That's another $420 which can be directly added to a mortgage payment, enabling you to spend a total of $1,420 each month.

Rather than wait for a refund, after consultation with an accountant, increase the number of dependents claimed so that your employer withholds $420 less each month. Don't worry about having to verify the number. As long as the total is kept to ten or below and the number on your tax return is correct, the IRS turns a blind eye to the maneuver.

Now take out your mortgage book. Turn to the page that charts 10 percent fixed-rate mortgages. That's probably the best deal you'll be able to find. In the thirty-year term column pick out the number closest to your maximum monthly mortgage payment. Using the previous example, paying $1,420 monthly would equate to a loan of approximately $160,000.

The next step in the process is figuring in a down payment. Bankers are very strict about down payments today. A few years back many institutions were writing 90 or even 95 percent mortgages. Those days are over. Now borrowers need to put a minimum of 20 percent down on any house, at any price, anywhere. The math at this point is simple: 20 percent of $160,000 equals $32,000; which means you could afford to spend $192,000—if you can come up with the $32,000 down payment.

Raising the down payment has been, and remains, the biggest obstacle for most people wishing to buy a home. Many can't conceive of being able to come up with $32,000, especially not while trying to save six months' expenses as well. All I can tell you is to do everything, short of stealing. Go back to chapter 8, in which I discussed ways of raising cash in an emergency, and use the same techniques.

There's nothing wrong with borrowing the money for a down payment. Return to the nest and ask parents for a loan. Approach grandparents, siblings, aunts, uncles, cousins, and friends. Speak to your employer about a loan. Cash in your IRA or Keogh accounts. Don't feel bad: In the long run a home is a better source of retirement funds than a personal savings plan; and once the mortgage payments are comfortable, you can start socking money away again. Find out about drawing against your company's pension plan. Borrow against life insurance policies or stock portfolios. Sell assets. Do whatever you can to come up with the cash. If you fall a bit short of your goal, don't despair: You may be able to make it up during the price negotiation.

Home buyers have incredible leverage in a recession. Many sellers have just about given up hope and may be willing to go to extreme lengths to sell their homes. In order to figure out how far the seller may be willing to go, you need to know as much as possible about him or her. The broker might be of some help here. In a recession a serious buyer is a rare commodity. Brokers will do everything they can to keep you in their clutches, including passing along information about the seller.

Concentrate your investigative efforts on finding out how long the house has been on the market, why it's being sold, and how much time pressure the seller is under. Take the fruits of your research and store them away—they're secret weapons to be brought out only when needed. For now you're going to rely strictly on your understanding of the value of the home.

Despite all the varied and complicated theories of negotiating, and all the posturing and ego put on display, it's really just salami slicing. The price a seller initially puts on his house is higher than he expects to receive. In response, your first offer will be lower than you're actually willing to pay. Bit by ever-decreasing bit, the two parties move toward a compromise position, or else one of them refuses to compromise and the negotiation ends. That doesn't mean the process is without science or subtlety.

The science comes in understanding the innate desire among unsophisticated negotiators to "split the difference." The assumption that accompanies a buyer's first offer is that she's willing to settle for the midpoint between the initial price and her offer. For example, if a home is listed at $250,000 and a buyer offers $200,000 in response, it indicates a willingness to settle on $225,000. The same holds true for the seller's counteroffer. Once again, it indicates an acceptable midpoint. If the seller in this scenario responds with a price of $245,000, it means he'll accept $235,000.

Understanding the urge to split the difference allows you to manipulate the numbers to your advantage, forcing the midpoint down as low as possible. Let's continue with the same example. In response to the seller's counteroffer of $245,000, an aggressive negotiator would respond in kind with an offer of $205,000. This keeps the midpoint at $225,000, rather than raising it to $235,000.

The subtle part of this sophisticated salami slicing is the presentation. You never want to appear to be assailing the seller's price or the quality of his home. Have a reason for every offer and concession you make, preferably citing some outside authority or expert. This demonstrates your logical approach to the process. Back up your initial offer, for example, by noting that an appraiser has told you that recent sales were all around $200,000, and explain your subsequent increase to $205,000 by saying you won't need to paint right away.

Throughout the process, commiserate with and flatter the seller. Explain how you know it must be difficult to sell such a lovely home, and it must be doubly painful to do so in a recession. Add, however, that you're in a recession, too, and have limited financial resources, even when it comes to purchasing his magnificent home. Savvy buyers will let the seller save face and make him feel his home will be "in good hands."

There are subtle ways to fan the flames of seller anxiety. If, for example, the seller is particularly eager to close the deal quickly, slow the negotiating process down. Insist that all offers be conveyed by intermediaries. Use the smallest increments you can in increasing your offers. Then make sure the exchanges only take place at the end of the day or, better yet, the end of the week. This may get the clock ticking loudly enough in the seller's head that he caves in and makes substantial concessions.

Subtlety can even help you soothe hurt feelings. Let's say the seller is insulted by the initial offer of $200,000, or the subsequent offer of $205,000, and refuses to respond. Rather than automatically boosting your offer—in effect bidding against yourself—simply state your willingness to negotiate. Tell the seller you're serious about buying his home and are willing to work out a deal with him, but that he must also be willing to compromise.

When the two of you start getting close, or appear to have reached an impasse, it's time to pull out your secret weapon: recession-induced seller desperation. Tell the seller you'll agree to his most recent offer, but in exchange you need his help to finance the deal. The possible scenarios are endless. For example, ask him to give you a three- or five-year, no-interest loan for the difference between your last offer and the selling price. What you're basically doing is agreeing to his price, but asking him to wait three to five years for some of the money. The loan should be guaranteed by your parents, or secured by their home rather than the home you're buying, since most primary-mortgage lenders will be scared off by a second mortgage. When the loan comes due, you can either refinance it with the seller, pay it off with cash, or take out another loan. In any case you'll have made out well.

In fact, anyone who buys a home during this recession should consider herself a success. This market is an opportunity that comes along only once a decade. And if you can take advantage of it, you'll have gotten a leg up on the rest of your financial life.

AFFORDABILITY WORKSHEET

1. Amount currently being spent on shelter each month $_____

2. Total give-ups $_____

3. Maximum rent (line 1 plus line 2) $_____

4. Marginal tax bracket _____%

5. Tax-deductibility benefit (line 3 multiplied by line 4) $_____

6. Maximum mortgage payment (line 3 plus line 5) $_____

7. Size of mortgage that maximum mortgage payment will allow you to borrow (as determined by mortgage chart) $_____

8. Size of desired down payment (line 7 multiplied by 20 percent) $_____

9. How much you can afford to spend on a home (line 7 plus line 8) $_____

CHAPTER 13

Investing Your Money Wisely

Though mothers and fathers give us life,
it is money alone which preserves it.
—Ihara Saikaku

This recession has disrupted everyone's financial life. Your net worth is probably less today than it was before the recession, especially if, like most Americans, a large portion of it consisted of real estate. Your stream of income has either been disastrously reduced—if you've had the misfortune to lose your job—or it has had its growth slowed to a crawl. All the recent debt-related upheavals have, I hope, changed your attitude toward borrowing and leverage. Some of the investments in which you were so confident back in the 1980s may have turned sour. Many of the go-go industries and hot companies of the 1980s have been hamstrung either by leveraged buyouts or by their inability to compete in today's tougher markets. And all indications are that they won't stabilize until well after the recession has faded into the past.

As a result of all this turmoil the goal timetable you'd drawn up for your life has either been side-tracked or made moot. While the economy was booming, your short-term goals seemed well within reach.

Today, however, they've drifted farther from your grasp, or at best have been frozen in place. For example, now that it's clear that real estate will no longer increase in value at as meteoric a rate, rather than looking for a starter home you could sell in three to five years, you're looking for a more substantial, and expensive, home you'll be able to live in for at least ten to fifteen years. Economic changes such as this require you to put long-term goals on the back burner. It's enough to make you lose faith in the American economy.

But don't let the recession sour you on investing in capitalism. The American economy is fundamentally sound. When agricultural and manufactured products are combined, the United States remains the world's leading exporter. All the gloomy statements about our becoming an industrial wasteland are overstated. We are still the number-one exporter of computers, aircraft, and heavy machinery. And despite what critics say, we produce more goods and services per worker and per hour than any other nation in the world. If you need any further proof of the inherent strength of capitalism, look to the recent events in Eastern Europe. As the curtain comes down on the twentieth century, it's clear that capitalism does the best job of enhancing the material welfare of the largest number of people. And because its basis is individual decision making, it's the system most compatible with individual freedom.

Rather than losing faith or giving up, use this recession as an opportunity to take a fresh look at your investment life and goals. In previous chapters I've helped you make sure your money was safe. Together we've tried to ensure that your stream of income was secure, whether it came from a job or your own business. We've checked the health of the underpinnings of your financial life: your bank, insurer, and pension fund. Now it's time to figure out how to manage your financial life from now on.

In chapter 5 I urged you to accumulate a six-month cash reserve. Since then you've probably been so obsessed with saving that you haven't given much thought to where you should be investing that money as it accumulated. If you're like most of us, the money's been stashed in a bank money market fund—the modern-day equivalent of hiding it under a mattress. The rate of interest on the fund allowed you to keep pace with inflation. But that's not enough: It's time to take the next step and get the money working for you.

I'm sure you're a little nervous about pulling those hard-earned bills out from their hiding place and exposing them to the perils of the investment world, but trust me, I won't let you put them in jeopardy. All we're going to do is earn as much interest on the money as possible while keeping it safe and liquid.

During this recession interest rates parallel the slumping economy. As the recession worsens, interest rates are being forced lower in an effort to stimulate economic growth. The theory is that once borrowing becomes more affordable, businesses and consumers start buying again, sparking an economic recovery. Unfortunately as interest rates drop, the money market fund where you've stashed the cash reserve becomes an increasingly poor place, since the rate it pays drops as well. In exchange for being able to draw the money out at a moment's notice, you get an increasingly lower return. What you need to do is to start investing the money in different vehicles and for slightly longer periods of time so that you can lock in higher rates of return.

I'm not suggesting you sock it away in a three-year

CD. You still need to keep this money liquid, but you don't need to have all of it instantly available. If, heaven forbid, you're faced with an emergency, you won't need to draw all the money out in the first month. At worst, as each month ensues, you'll need to draw another month's worth of expenses. That means you can stagger the maturities of the investments and still have it readily available for the emergency. This can be accomplished by putting the money into a variety of different investments, including short-term CDs, government bonds and notes, mutual funds that deal with short-term municipal bonds, and other quality instruments.

The secret is continually to roll over the short-term investments that contain your six-month fund in order to maximize their yield while maintaining relative liquidity. This can get a little complicated, since it requires that you investigate and reinvest some money nearly every month. Instead I recommend that my clients place at least five months of their six-month reserve in what's commercially called an asset management account. These accounts, managed by major brokerage and investment firms, take care of all this continual reinvesting. While they charge a slight fee, I think it's worth it when you consider how much time it saves you and how much more efficient these firms are at determining the correct short-term investments for your money.

Now that you've established a cash reserve and have maximized its yield, give yourself a much-deserved pat on the back: You've accomplished something many Americans only dream of. Don't become complacent, however. There's no going back to the spending habits of the past. The 1980s are over, and so are the days of instant gratification and living wastefully. You've been able to go this long without going out to dinner twice a week or buying a new wardrobe every season, and now isn't the time to start again. I'm not saying you should adopt the depression-era philosophy of my parents, in which borrowing and spending were mortal sins, but neither can you return to the inflation-era philosophy of the 1970s and 1980s, in which saving and sacrifice were vices, not virtues. We must all seek out a compromise philosophy, in which we use leverage as a powerful tool to better our lives—to buy or renovate a home, start a business, or pay for a college education—while remaining fully aware of how addictive it can be. And rather than relying on debt to finance our futures, we must begin to fund ourselves. That means continuing to save money whenever possible. As the dollars begin to accumulate—and they will—you'll be carefully investing them to best achieve your goals.

In order to develop savvy investment strategies, it's important to review your priorities and goals. Many of us formulated our goals believing that incomes would always outpace inflation and that homes would dramatically increase in value each and every year. In the mid-1980s you may have made the purchase of a vacation home your main long-term goal, believing that the value of your current home would increase enough for it to become a source of your retirement fund. Since we now know that real estate won't continue to soar in price as rapidly as it did in the past ten years, accumulating money for retirement must take on a new vigor. I'm not saying you should give up your dreams. I agree with Robert Browning: A person's reach should exceed his grasp. But it's time to become more realistic about the timing surrounding those goals. You may be able to achieve everything you desire, but it won't all come as quickly as you may have thought in past years. Today you must decide which of your objectives is the most important.

Divide your objectives into short- and long-term goals. Short-term goals are those things you wish to accomplish in the next three to five years. Long-term goals are those that are more than five years down the road. Where various life goals fall depends on your age and personal circumstances. For example, if you have a very young child or there's one on the way, paying for his or her college education may be among the long-term goals. But if the child is already in his teens, paying for a college education may be a short-term goal. If you have two children, college funding could be both a short- and long-term goal. Retirement funds are a little simpler: Establishing one is a long-term objective for everyone under the age of fifty. Then it turns into a short-term goal.

Obviously the purchase of a home can be either a short- or a long-term goal, depending on your circumstances. But what separates home buying from other goals, and what makes it, in my opinion, a priority objective, is that it can also be viewed as a long-term investment. When you buy a home, not only do you satisfy a need for shelter and better your life, but you also add a growing asset to your net worth; an asset that can later be used as a source for retirement funds, seed capital for a business, maybe even college-education funds. However, that's really an added bonus. No one should buy a home solely as an investment. Alternatively there are three basic investment strategies you could follow: Make debt investment, equity investments, or both.

When you acquire a debt investment, you're loaning someone else money and receiving in exchange evidence of the loan, which carries with it the promise to pay the loan back at a specified time, with a prearranged rate of interest. There are many different forms of debt investments or securities, but the most common are notes, bonds, certificates of deposit, money market funds, passbook savings accounts, and debt-based mutual funds. The advantage of a debt investment is its predictability. The disadvantage is there's a ceiling on your earnings. You know exactly how much you'll be receiving and when, but that's all you'll ever receive. I agree with most money managers that debt investments are the perfect tools for financing your short-term goals. If you need $25,000 in five years, by purchasing the appropriate debt instrument you guarantee the money will be there when you need it.

An equity investment is anything you take ownership of, fully or partly, with the hope that it increases in value. Equity investments include commercial real estate, stocks, and equity-based mutual funds. The advantages of prudently selected equity investments are that they will substantially grow in value, and there's absolutely no limit on how high the value can go. The disadvantage is there's no set timetable for how long it will take for the value to rise to the level you desire. Sound equity investments give you the potential for incredible growth over a long period of time, making them, I believe, the ideal vehicle for achieving your long-term goals.

Sounds simple enough: Invest enough in debt securities to meet your short-term goals and after they're achieved, invest the balance in equity instruments for your long-term goals. Theoretically that's right, but it doesn't take into account the organic nature of your financial life. You'll never actually be able to free yourself from short-term goals, and, at least up until very old age, you'll always have long-term goals as well. That means you'll always want to have a combination of debt and equity investments so that you get some guaranteed short-term returns while still building up long-term value. Rather than a simple two-step process of starting with debt investments and then moving on to equity investments, you must actually divide your investments between debt and equity, or short-term and long-term.

The actual division of your investments between debt and equity depends on your age, your life circumstances, and your willingness to take risks. A young person, for example, might put more of her money into equity than debt investments since she has more long-term goals than short-term goals and, due to her youth, can take a few more chances with her money since she has more time to recoup losses. An older person, on the other hand, may put more of his money into debt rather than equity since he should have fewer long-term goals and needs to be safer with his investments. But there really are no hard-and-fast rules.

I have clients who are the twin sons of a very wealthy couple. Both were given substantial sums of money on their twenty-first birthdays. And despite being the same age and having the same amount of money, I've advised them differently. One son is in graduate school while the other has an excellent job. The student's priority is income to support himself while finishing school. We've invested 60 percent of his money in debt and 40 percent in equity. His twin's monies are invested in the exact reverse manner—40 percent in debt and 60 percent in equity—since his income is quite sizable and his long-term goals far outweigh his short-term ones in importance.

Sometimes the divisions aren't so clear-cut. Along with the myriad of straight-debt and straight-equity investments, those wishing to hedge their bets can look to financial instruments that combine elements of debt and equity into a single hybrid package. There are corporate bonds that can be converted into corporate stock. Shares of preferred stock, while equity investments, also carry cash dividend tickets assuring a specific return.

There are other permutations and twists as well. Bonds can be either callable or noncallable. At a time of low interest, the company or municipality that has borrowed money and issued a callable bond can elect to pay it off and obtain another loan from the market at the new, more advantageous interest rate, while the company or municipality that has issued a noncallable bond cannot pay it off before its maturity date. And let's not forget that debt investments can be totally taxable, partially taxable, or tax-free, affecting both the interest it pays and of course the yield you receive.

If you think things are beginning to get complicated, you're right. I believe the financial world has become too confusing for a person to be able sift through and make an intelligent choice without spending full time on the job. And unless you're already financially independent, most of your time is devoted to working for a living rather than studying the financial markets and reading hundreds of different prospectuses. While I'm able to help my clients decide on strategies for their money, I can't possibly keep up with the thousands of products available. Once it's time to invest money and select products, I send them to someone who's an expert in the field. Often that expert is a certified financial planner, though it can be any financial adviser who charges a fee for her services.

The financial-planning profession emerged to fill a gap in expertise. Accountants, while knowledgeable on tax matters, are often ignorant of the wealth of investment options available. Attorneys, skilled in deciphering the legal and contractual aspects of investments, may not be financially astute. And sellers of investments, such as stockbrokers or bonds salesmen, while thoroughly versed in products, earn their money on commission, leading them to be biased advisers. Salespeople neither discourage purchasing nor steer a potential customer to someone else's product. A financial adviser who charges an hourly fee for her services rather than relying on commission is the best possible adviser in selecting products.

Get the names of some reliable advisers from your accountant, attorney, and banker. Stress that you're looking for someone who charges an hourly consultation fee rather than just selling products. If the planner you used back in chapter 4 to check on the health of your financial foundations did a good job, add her name to the list. Look for independent planners or those who work for small firms. The larger financial-planning practices often specialize in putting together extremely sophisticated packages for very wealthy people. You want someone who has experience working with people who have incomes similar to your own. In addition, try to limit your candidates to those planners who have more than just financial-planning credentials. Since the field is relatively young and its codes of standards and ethics are still being formed, added licenses or educational degrees can serve as a safety net. Stick with planners who are also attorneys, CPAs, or who have an MBA degree in finance.

Schedule an interview with each planner on your list. In addition to looking for signs of professionalism, try to get a sense for the rapport between the planner and yourself. To some extent, selecting a financial planner is more like choosing an architect than a financial professional. Sure, you want the planner to know everything there is to know about money, but you also want someone who listens closely to what you say and don't say and who seems to have your interests at heart. The goal of a good financial planner is to obtain as large a yield on your money as possible, without keeping you awake at night. Beware of planners who ask you to take standardized money-attitude tests. These questionnaires are actually designed to determine what you'd be more apt to buy, not what's best for you. You want a planner who relies on speaking with you and getting a feeling for your unique situation, goals, and risk aversion, rather than someone who looks to pigeonhole you in order to make his job easier.

Stress to the planner your desire to pursue a blended investment plan. If the three golden rules of real estate are location, location, and location, the corresponding rules for investing are diversity, diversity, and diversity. The more you blend your investments across the entire stock or debt market, for example, the safer they are. Granted, by selecting a specific stock or bond you could get a much higher yield, but you could also lose money.

There are industries, for example, that have a history of doing well in the year following a recession. Airlines, home construction, leisure products, trucking, and publishing are a few of the often-cited examples. But I don't believe that that alone is a reason to buy stock in them. By doing so you're treating the purchase of stock as a short- rather than a long-term investment. The stocks you pick may well go up in value right after the recession, but they could drop the year later, and you'll never know if they've peaked and you should sell them until they start falling.

Buying shares in a mutual stock fund, on the other hand, allows you to add your handful of dollars to an enormous pool that is being spread across a segment of the entire market. The potential rewards are less, but so are the risks. There are, of course, degrees of blending as well. Some mutual funds, for example, concentrate on companies in a particular industry, or municipal debt securities from particular regions. Buying into them may be a good compromise for those willing to take a discrete measure of risk but who fear putting all their eggs into one basket.

If you buy shares in a particular drug company because you've heard it's the farthest along in developing a cure for Alzheimer's disease, or a specific home renovation retailer because it does the best job of selling goods profitably, you're taking a definite risk. If you buy shares in a mutual fund that concentrates in health care companies because the population in general is aging and needs more health care, or home improvement companies because more and more people are renovating their homes, you're taking a lesser risk. If you choose simply to invest in a mutual fund made up of blue-chip stocks in a variety of industries, you're taking very little risk.

While your financial adviser can help analyze how best to divide your investments and suggest in which products to actually invest, that doesn't mean you should just reflexively accept her judgments. A financial planner, like any other professional, is at best an adviser. The final responsibility is yours. You wouldn't sign a contract your lawyer has prepared without examining it, or a tax return your CPA has filled out without first checking it. And neither should you invest in something your planner has recommended without first reading the prospectus.

By federal and state law any security offered for public sale must provide certain information to potential investors. Generally this information is included, along with a sales pitch, in a document called a prospectus. While the law stipulates what information must be made available, it says nothing about how it should be presented or where. Important disclosures may be summarized on the cover, listed in fine print on an inside page, or hidden in minuscule footnotes. That's why, even though it's not the most stimulating reading, a savvy consumer reads through an entire prospectus looking for important information. For a list of what items to look for in a prospectus, see page 216.

The first item to check is the date of the prospectus. You'd be amazed at how often people base an investment decision on an old prospectus. Next look for a formal statement of the investment's objective and a discussion of what restrictions or limitations it has placed on its behavior. Obviously you're trying to see if your and the investment's goals coincide.

Turn to the risk section of the prospectus and ferret out information on the investment's key officers, its potential litigation problems, any conflicts of interest, and the size of its customer base or source of supply. Are there one or two individuals who are vital for the investment's success; and if there are, have plans been made to compensate for their loss? Does the investment have any current or pending claims against it that could effect its financial health? Do there appear to be any negative conflicts of interest? How dependent is the investment on a limited number of customers and/or suppliers; and what would happen to the investment if there were problems with them?

Take a good long look at the performance section of the prospectus. In an effort to make it easier to compare the performances of mutual funds, the Securities and Exchange Commission requires them all to follow a standard formula. But other investments aren't bound by the requirement, and it's easy to get confused by all the financial jargon, charts, footnotes, and numbers being thrown about. There are just a handful of simple facts you need to sort out from all the puffery. First find the net-income figure to make sure the investment actually is profitable. Then divide the net income by the number of shares outstanding so that you've an idea of how much profit you're purchasing along with your share. Next look for information on the investment's cash position. Has it been increasing or decreasing; and why? If cash has been shrinking, perhaps there's a problem with liquidity, or maybe management has been drawing excessive salaries. Increases in cash are great, as long as they're not the result of too much borrowing. Check the footnotes carefully—they're a great place to hide bad news. And above all remember that this is indicative of past performance, which may or may not predict future performance.

Just as you wouldn't loan money to a total stranger, so you shouldn't make an investment without first studying who's managing the money. The credentials, abilities, and past performance of the investment's management team should be completely spelled out in the prospectus. Study it carefully. Check to see how long the manager has been with this investment. In the case of a mutual fund the manager is vital. When a new manager is brought in, you can throw all past performance figures—positive or negative—out the window.

Try to determine why money is being solicited from people at this time. Does the investment plan to expand or acquire another property? Does it desperately need cash to pay off big debts? Or maybe the current shareholders want to sell out; if so, why? Be especially wary of vague claims about needing the money for "general corporate purposes." The more specific the need, the better.

Finally study the fees. You can generally find a summary of them in a box or chart in the first few pages of the prospectus. Determine how much they are and when they must be paid. Some investments charge all fees up front, others spread them throughout the course of the investment, and still others wait until the investment is dissolved before assessing them.

If the proposed investment is a more seasoned entity, such as a long-established company, its prospectus will be outdated. In that case you must study its history. This can be done by reading through recent annual reports, its Standard & Poors profile (obtainable at public libraries), and articles that have appeared in the business press.

If ever you come across something troubling and incomprehensible in the prospectus or your research, ask your adviser about it. If she can explain it to your satisfaction, fine; if not, don't invest. It's your money, not the adviser's, being put on the line. And while that entitles you to reap the rewards, it also requires you to take the risks.

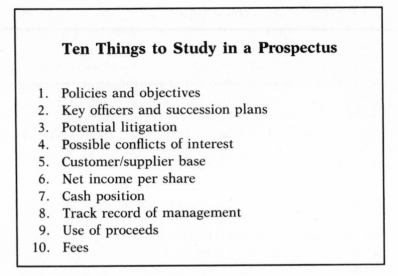

Ten Things to Study in a Prospectus

1.   Policies and objectives
2.   Key officers and succession plans
3.   Potential litigation
4.   Possible conflicts of interest
5.   Customer/supplier base
6.   Net income per share
7.   Cash position
8.   Track record of management
9.   Use of proceeds
10. Fees

CHAPTER 14

Starting Your Own Company

Launching your own business is like writing your own personal declaration of independence from the corporate beehive, where you sell bits of your life in forty-hour (or longer) chunks in return for a paycheck. . . . Going into business for yourself, becoming an entrepreneur, is the modern-day equivalent of pioneering on the old frontier.
—Paula Nelson

Americans have an almost indigenous desire to go into business for themselves. Nearly every one of us wants to be his own boss. We see entrepreneurship as an escape from the employer whims and tyranny and a chance to achieve true financial independence and freedom. The recession has done nothing to diminish this desire and in some ways has made the urgency even greater. Massive layoffs have shown the compact between employer and employee to be not only unwritten but in many cases nonexistent. And our current financial insecurity only reinforces the importance of fiscal independence.

This recession has not only buttressed the arguments in favor of entrepreneurship but it has opened up a host of new opportunities as well. There's actually a convergence of economic factors that make this recession the perfect time to go into business for yourself. A whole host of new business and consumer needs is developing. Many existing businesses are so busy trying to stay afloat and hold on to their old customers that they have no time to pursue these opportunities. That leaves the door open for entrepreneurs. And while these new needs may have been spawned by the current economic downturn, financial and demographic trends point to them continuing on well into the future. Businesses that target these new needs are therefore just about ensured of a long, potentially prosperous life span.

I know what you're thinking: Two of your primary personal financial goals—minimizing debt and remaining liquid—seem to run contrary to pursuing entrepreneurship. There are ways to split the difference, however. It's possible to launch a business without taking on excessive debt and while keeping your finances liquid—all it takes is selecting the right method to do it. But before we get into ways of going into business, let's examine the new opportunities that are available.

Businesses of all sizes are in the process of streamlining operations. With the recession cutting into revenue and tightening up credit, companies are trimming support staff right and left. Recognizing it's cheaper to pay retainage or hourly fees than to employ staff people, organizations that once had in-house legal and accounting departments are now hiring outside professional advisers. Public relations, art, design, and training staffs are being dismantled as firms seek to eliminate positions. Some corporations are even looking for outside secretarial, bookkeeping, photocopying, and maintenance services in an effort to trim labor costs. This opens up a world of opportunities for entrepreneurs who can provide consulting, free-lance, or part-time services to businesses. Ironically many middle managers who have been laid off are starting their own businesses and selling their services back to the company that terminated them.

In response to this trend one client of mine launched a company that supplies temporary white-collar workers for businesses. He selected California as the best place to locate the business, since at the time the recession hadn't yet reached there, and he wanted his operation to be in place before the full effects of the economic downturn were felt. As the new guy in town, he was able to position his business perfectly, targeting his marketing directly at those companies that were just beginning to thin their payrolls. Needless to say the business has been a tremendous success. He's currently three months ahead of his projected growth schedule. And by the time the recession is over, he will have carved out a sizable share of the market.

In addition to streamlining staff, businesses are trimming the number and range of products and services offered. Where once a company sought to provide its customers with a full menu, now it's dropping sidelines and becoming a provider of only its basic and most profitable items. Instead of producing all types of footwear, for example, a shoe manufacturer may today be concentrating on work boots since they're its most profitable line. A computer software company, rather than offering every type of business software imaginable for every kind of business, is now centering its efforts on one type of software or one type of business. A sporting-goods retailer is probably no longer carrying clothing, footwear, camping products, and athletic supplies, dropping those parts of the package where margins are the lowest. An astute entrepreneur can step into the breach and pick up the sideline businesses others are dropping, using his or her newness and small size to turn a profit on products or services that weren't profitable for a larger, more established business.

The economic pressures of the recession are forcing increasing numbers of American families to become two-income households. And once back on the job they're finding there's no time clock in the 1990s. If they want to keep their job and move ahead, they must put in long hours. That means they've little or no time to take care of all the mundane but necessary tasks of daily living. To make matters even more pressing, many of these households now contain young children or elderly parents who need care. Meanwhile the number of single-parent families and households with only one occupant are rising as well. All these consumers are in desperate need of goods and services that help them save time or make the most of the little time they have. For savvy entrepreneurs these people represent a potential gold mine. Food shopping, house cleaning, pick up and delivery, errand running, laundry, cooking, child care, and elder-care services will all boom today and for years to come.

Economic pressures are also forcing both businesses and consumers to think twice about expensive purchases and to consider repairing rather than replacing big-ticket items. When the economy is tight, small entrepreneurial businesses that repair things, or that help consumers repair things themselves, do well. And since all indications are that salaries won't be rising any time soon, this new frugality will probably be around for quite some time.

In addition to the development of these new needs, there's a general demographic trend that makes entrepreneurship even more viable. Where once American consumers made up a relatively homogeneous mass market—father worked, mother stayed in the suburban home with two kids and a dog—in the 1980s they broke up into smaller market segments. Two of the most widely cited new markets were baby-boomers and older Americans. In response to the segmentation of the mass market, American businesses began offering more and different products, in a wider variety of sizes and styles, and with a bigger range of prices.

As we enter the 1990s, the segmented consumer market is breaking up into even smaller pieces. Baby-boomers, for example, can now be divided into white-collar baby-boomers without children, white-collar baby-boomers with children, blue-collar baby-boomers without children, blue-collar baby-boomers with children, baby-boomer couples that are just starting out, baby-boomers who are single, and so on. Even the elderly, once thought to be all sedentary retirees, are now viewed as being a diverse group. There are the healthy and active elderly, the healthy but inactive elderly, the ailing but active elderly, and the ailing and inactive elderly, to name just four of the microsegments. Such increasingly narrow market groups play to the entrepreneur's strength.

In order for a large company to be profitable, it must use its size to achieve economies of scale. In other words, big companies thrive on volume. That's great when you can produce one or a handful of products and with them address the needs of all consumers. But as consumer needs become more diverse, a wider variety of products are necessary, and economies of scale are lost. Smaller companies, which tend to be entrepreneurial businesses, are better able to address the specific needs of smaller markets.

For instance, a company that prints a magazine for photographers may find the market for a general photographic publication shrinking as the audience becomes more diverse. Rather than try to be all things to all photographers, it may choose to stick with those whom it perceives to be the bulk of the market, let's say photo hobbyists. This presents a chance to produce more specialized publications for the smaller market segments abandoned or ignored by the larger company. A savvy entrepreneur could respond by launching newsletters directed toward travel photography and child photography and aimed at snap-shooters rather than hobbyists.

Clearly opportunities for new businesses abound. But how can you start one without taking on dangerously high levels of debt or losing your financial liquidity? There are two answers: You can base the business in your home, or you can buy an already existing business.

Increasing numbers of Americans are finding the home-based business an appealing option. While estimates on the number of home entrepreneurs are cloudy, the best guess is that about thirteen million full- or part-time businesses are currently being operated from homes. Projections on future growth are also hazy, but experts I've spoken with seem to agree that one out of every five Americans will work from his or her home by the year 2000—either as an entrepreneur or as a telecommuter. The vast majority of these people are motivated by the life-style advantages of home business. They see it as the perfect way to improve or maintain their family life and career simultaneously. And with some reservations—home entrepreneurship isn't a solution to the child-care dilemma—I agree. But home entrepreneurship is more than just a life-style choice.

A home location drastically reduces the start-up and operating costs of a business. What for many businesses is their largest monthly operating cost—rent—is transformed from a financial drain into a tax advantage. Normally only the interest portion of your monthly home mortgage payment is deductible. But when you conduct a business from your home, you're able to deduct a portion of the principle as well. If, for example, your home office occupies one-quarter of the total square footage of the home, one-quarter of the entire mortgage payment is tax deductible through the business. Leasehold improvement and insurance expenses can also be significantly reduced by locating the business in the home. In addition, the sizable deposits landlords often require of commercial tenants are eliminated, dramatically reducing the need for start-up funds. While you'll obviously need to spend some money—for things such as equipment and furniture—a home location can mean the difference between having to take out a sizable personal loan or just using your credit cards. That's why I'm encouraging my entrepreneur clients to give serious consideration to starting a business from their home, regardless of the life-style considerations. In a recession, when money is hard to find and debt is extremely dangerous, a home location—even if only temporarily—can be the solution. It can get you into business now, when the opportunities are greatest.

An added bonus is that the home location actually lends itself to answering many of the new needs of businesses and consumers. Any operation that has as its main resource the skill and knowledge of the entrepreneur—such as those that offer advice and services to businesses—can be run easily from the home. Since all a consultant actually needs is a telephone, chair, desk, computer, and fax machine, it can be just as easily be located in a spare bedroom as in a downtown office suite. In addition, any business that offers home-related services to consumers—such as housekeeping, shopping, and in-home child care or elder care—needs only a telephone, a file cabinet, and a place to store supplies and equipment, since most of the operations will take place at remote locations.

Of course there's nothing that limits you to operating only a service business from your home. Technology has progressed to the point where almost any type of business operation can be run with a personal computer and telephone. And while there are legal restrictions on the business use of a home, ingenious entrepreneurs can work around them. Rather than operate a store, a home entrepreneur/retailer can launch a mail-order or catalog business, for example.

Even though such innovations tend to be the rule with home-based enterprises, it's important for individuals who choose this route into business to follow sound entrepreneurial practices. Your operation will still need to address existing needs, prepare a business plan, maintain sufficient operating capital, and install a record-keeping and financial system. Most important of all, you'll need to come up with a suitable marketing plan.

Home-based businesses, whatever their inherent advantages, face an image problem. For many potential clients—whether consumers or businesses themselves—a firm being based in a home connotes that it's somehow less substantial. While this is changing, the overriding perception is that is that entrepreneurs launch a business from their home because they have no other option. Even the most enlightened corporate executive feels that a formal office setting symbolizes legitimacy and permanence. Counteracting this outdated attitude is the major challenge facing home-based entrepreneurs.

Every public demonstration by a home-based entrepreneur, including her appearance, stationery, and answering-machine message, must be a formal and traditional as they would be if the business were being operated out of an orthodox location. Since many service businesses involve frequent client consultations, home-based entrepreneurs should, whenever possible, arrange meetings at the customer's location. When that's not possible, meetings should be scheduled at neutral locations, such as restaurants, private clubs, or hotels. While I don't recommend lying to clients, the home location can be disguised through the use of post office boxes and private mail drops. If a client ever questions the legitimacy of your business due to its being operated from a home, address the issue head-on. Explain that rather than being a detriment, it's actually a benefit, allowing you to maintain lower operating costs, which are in turn reflected in your fees.

If you can't run your company from the home, another way to become an entrepreneur during a recession is to buy an existing business. While buying someone else's business may not fit the classic definition or common image of being an entrepreneur, it has a great many advantages. It's much less of a gamble than starting from scratch, since along with the physical assets of the business, you're buying something that has a proven track record, an established customer base, and, hopefully, goodwill. Most important of all, when you buy a business, you've a built-in, flexible lender—the previous owner.

Rather than rushing out and investigating businesses that are up for sale—and there are many available due to the economic downturn—decide first what type of business you're interested. No matter how reasonable the price, a business that doesn't fit your unique skills, abilities, and personality, or match up with current consumer and business needs isn't worth buying. Remember, every business that is up for sale is being sold for a reason. And while it might be that the owner/operator has recently died, or is aging and has no heirs, it's more than likely there's something wrong with the business. There are some wonderful opportunities out there to purchase failing or failed businesses for pennies on the dollar, particularly if you can buy them directly from bankers who may also be willing to provide you with financing, but there's still the risk of buying a dog. That's why I generally recommend that my clients steer clear of businesses that are up for sale and instead try to convince an owner to sell. It's not as difficult as it sounds.

Everyone, especially an entrepreneur, has a price. By their very nature entrepreneurs are project- rather than process-oriented. They thrive on creation, not maintenance. The typical entrepreneur starts multiple businesses in her lifetime. Some succeed and others fail, but all have limited life spans, since an entrepreneur's attention and interest are always attracted to new challenges. Apply all the techniques, insight, and skills involved in deciding what type of business to start and where to locate it, to ferreting out businesses that would be good to buy. Once you've come across one that fits the bill, approach the owner and offer him the opportunity for a lifelong income. That will be sure to get his attention. From this point on, the task gets more even more complicated.

Determining the value of an active business is a very complex process, involving estimates not only of its physical assets but of its current and future revenue-generating potential. Since most businesses do everything possible to minimize profits when filing taxes, returns and formal records aren't accurate measurements. Rather than rely on owner assurances, you must enlist the help of an experienced team of professional advisers consisting of an accountant, attorney, and business appraiser. They'll know what to investigate and which formulas to apply in coming up with an offer.

Even with such professional guidance, establishing the value of a business and setting a purchase price are subjective processes based to a large degree on the promises and assurances of the current owner. It's this subjective nature of the buy, however, that makes it possible to use the seller as the source of funds. That makes the negotiation between buyer and seller at least as important as the actual dollar amount. In exchange for accepting the seller's figures, you'll be asking him to take back a mortgage on the business itself and to help finance the purchase. But the negotiation doesn't end there.

To further reduce the purchase price, you and your professional team can add myriad elements to the transactions. For example, while you want to purchase the assets of the business, you don't have to take ownership of its liabilities. Rather than simply buying the operation's balance sheet, you want the previous owner to retain responsibility for his past actions. You don't want to be held liable for his debts, past tax returns, or any lawsuits resulting from things done prior to your taking ownership. That means the transaction must be set up so that the previous owner can actually dissolve the business and then sell the assets of the now-defunct company to you. Obviously this is a paper process and won't affect the actual operations of the business.

You can also thin out the business's assets before the purchase. Instead of taking ownership of real estate, equipment, and fixtures, you can have the seller rent or lease them to you. Similarly accounts receivable can remain with the seller, guaranteeing him additional income while freeing you of the responsibility for collection. If the business rents rather than owns its location, your purchase contract can be made contingent on getting a rent reduction. And if the owner has any specific requests—such as keeping a relative on staff or maintaining the company name—these can also be used as leverage.

If the seller is unable or unwilling to go along with these attempts at reducing the price, consider structuring the deal as an "earnout." You can agree, in principle, to pay the seller's asking price, but structure the deal so that payment is tied to the business's ability to generate the kinds of profits the seller claims. Let's say the book value of a business (the value of its tangible assets) is $25,000, but the seller is asking $100,000. You can give the $25,000 as an initial payment but require that further payments be linked to the performance of the business. If the seller states that the business generates $5,000 in profit each month, it should be able to generate $150,000 in profits in thirty months. Therefore why not offer the seller 50 percent of the business's profits for the next thirty months. If the business lives up to the seller's claims, he'll receive his asking price. If it fails to meet expectations, he'll receive less. In any case you'll have been able to have the business pay for itself.

Five Rules for Establishing a Home Office

1. Avoid remodeling and renovation—the cost reduces the inherent financial advantage of a home location.
2. While compromises are necessary, the best possible home office would be at least 144 square feet; well lit; outside the normal flow of household traffic; cool in summer and warm in winter; near a bathroom; and far from the kitchen.
3. Do a cost-benefit analysis before buying any piece of equipment. Will it be more affordable to rent or lease rather than buy? Would using an outside service—for photocopying and facsimile transmissions, for example—make more sense?
4. Buy only what you currently need, not what you think you'll need in the future, and place the highest priority on durability and compactness.
5. Don't cut corners when selecting a chair. The cost will more than be made up in increased comfort and productivity.

CHAPTER 15

Expanding Your Business

Entrepreneurial profit . . . is the expression of the value of what the entrepreneur contributes to production in exactly the same sense that wages are the value expression of what the worker "produces." It is not a profit of exploitation any more than are wages.
—Joseph Alois Schumpeter

A business is never stagnant: it's either growing or dying. And this recession is really just a catalyst, increasing the rate of growth or decay. Those businesses that entered the recession weak, will emerge even weaker . . . or won't emerge at all. But businesses that entered the recession strong, or that strengthened themselves once it began, will, once it ends, find themselves healthier and in better shape than ever before. That's because the recession is like a discount store for savvy business people. Bargains are everywhere, and opportunities are just waiting to be exploited.

You can use the national economic decline to your advantage by becoming a more global company. If one dollar used to equal four French francs, and today it equals three, a French consumer can buy your product for 25 percent less. You've an automatic price advantage without having to cut your price. With the dollar weak overseas, American businesses have an excellent chance to make a dent in foreign markets. But there are also opportunities right here at home.

Larger companies, which sell multiple products and services, in an effort to better weather the recession are in the process of streamlining operations, eliminating from their offerings those items it sells in lesser numbers. This gives you a chance to expand your business into those markets that your larger competitors are abandoning.

A retail electronic chain, for example, may be thinning out its inventory of home-office equipment and refocusing on its core business of consumer-oriented products. If you're a smaller competitor, this gives you a chance to add those items to your inventory and address the market the large store is surrendering. While the home-office-equipment market may not offer enough volume to be worthwhile for a large operation, it could be perfect for you, since you don't need such sizable numbers.

Businesses, both large and small, are busy trimming costs. Invariably the first thing many cut is their marketing budget. With the noise level substantially lower, you've an excellent opportunity to make a big splash and get a larger share of the market. Whereas in the past you'd need to spend a great deal of money to stand out from the crowd, today, with your competitors reducing their marketing budgets, a big splash costs must less.

Let's say you own a small local clothing store. Your competitors are cutting back from running a full-page ad every week in the local paper to a half-page ad. If you maintain your full-page ad or, better yet, run an additional page, the further exposure more than makes up for the added cost, since it's multiplied by your competitors' diminished presence.

Be careful, however, not to cut your prices in this effort to gain market share. Both businesses and consumers today base their decisions on more than just price. While you may be able to gain a few new clients by cutting your fees, once the recession and peoples' temporary fixation on price ends, they'll probably head back to their original source. A better method would be to keep your prices level, increase your marketing, and emphasize the added value you offer in terms of quality or service. Any market share you gain in this manner will still be there when the economy improves.

Those businesses that aren't busy streamlining and cutting costs are going broke. This presents you with an even greater break. Owners of failing businesses are well aware that the value of the sum of the parts of their business is now greater than the value for the whole. As a result they'll be eager to sell off assets. During this recession you'll probably be able to buy raw materials, products for resale, parts, equipment, fixtures, customer lists, and even real estate cheaper than ever before.

If you owned a flourishing one-hour photo-processing lab, for instance, you might be able to buy new or additional equipment from a failing competitor at a fraction of what it would normally cost. You could stock up on cheap paper and chemicals from a supplier that is tottering on the brink of bankruptcy. It's possible you could even get the abandoned kiosk in the local shopping mall for a song.

Two clients of mine, partners in an aerobics studio, successfully exploited the bankruptcy of a nearby competitor. As soon as their rival went bust, the two enterprising young women plastered posters advertising their own studio all over the exterior of the now-closed studio. In addition they contacted the closed studio's instructors, offering them the chance to shift allegiances and bring their students with them. Thus far they've been able to pick up almost 80 percent of the competitor's business.

Another expansion alternative is to start or buy a secondary business. While it needn't be identical to your current operation, it should be complementary. That way you'll be able to incubate it by spreading your overhead and efforts across both businesses. (Reread chapter 14 for more information.)

I know what you're thinking. While all of these are great ideas, they cost money, something that is in very short supply right now. You're right, expanding your business requires additional dollars, which, unless you've been hoarding cash or came up with sizable savings back in chapter 3, you probably don't have. The answer is to go out and get it. And while banks and savings and loans are today about as eager to lend as they are to invite the examiner in for a thorough inspection of the books, there is money available. Raising money for business during a recession is like selling a home or getting a job: It's possible, but requires long hours, hard work, and some creativity.

The first thing to do is to determine how much, if any, additional debt you can afford to carry. With the help of your accountant, calculate how much more you would be able to pay in debt service each month, based of course on your future projected revenue after putting the loan to use. Try to combine your request for these funds with a renegotiation of existing loans, as I discussed back in chapter 3. If that's not possible, your best bet is to broaden the search for funds beyond the usual sources. If a banker who's already in partnership with you is hesitant to advance more money, it's unlikely that another banker will. Approach nonbank lenders, such as the financial divisions of major industrial corporations, as well as life insurance companies and the Small Business Administration. If need be, ask your suppliers to serve as a lender by extending more generous terms. Leave no stone unturned.

If all your efforts go for naught, don't give up. Just because lenders have turned you down doesn't mean you must give up your expansion plans. You can try to find investors instead. Perhaps now is the time to sell some of your equity in the business in exchange for the funds to expand.

Equity financing is actually essential for the long-term health of a business. When an enterprise relies solely on debt financing, all the profits it generates may end up having to go toward servicing its debt rather than being invested back in the business. What results is a death spiral, with the company continually borrowing to expand so that it can pay off previous loans. Of course the risk in equity financing is that along with partial ownership you're handing over partial control. But unless you have lots of cash readily available or have been underleveraged up to now, the only way you're going to be able to take advantage of the opportunities this recession offers is to sell off part of the business.

Probably the best way to obtain equity financing is to turn to family, friends, your professionals, your employees, and other private individuals and ask them to invest in your business, in effect becoming your partners. The advantage of such arrangements is that through carefully constructing the partnership agreements you ensure that control of your business remains in your own hands. Such deals can be structured in any number of ways in order to make them most attractive to investors. For example, a debt/equity hybrid arrangement that offers a set yearly dividend may help overcome objections from investors who are looking for their money to generate at least some income. The number of people you approach to become partners is limited only by the size of your Rolodex. (For ideas on how to expand your network, read chapter 11.)

If you can't scrape together enough funds from "friendly" investors, your other option is to turn to venture capitalists and small business investment corporations, their Small Business Administration–licensed counterparts. Both are in the business of investing in companies, such as yours, in exchange for a share in ownership. Most venture-capital deals contain a small debt element as well so that the investor can receive a regular income to cover administrative costs.

Venture capital is a very specialized field. Some firms are interested only in high-tech businesses, while others are on the lookout for retailers on the verge of expanding, so preliminary research is essential. Whatever their specialty, venture capitalists are primarily looking for a business that is about to grow rapidly and generate substantial profits. They're attracted to skilled entrepreneur/managers who have visions and plans of making those visions into realities.

The catch is that in exchange for investing in those visions they want a substantial return—sometimes as high as 30 percent. Obviously venture capitalists are more concerned with getting their return than in the continued health of your business. Their investment contracts generally contain what's called a "put" clause. At a certain point, hopefully defined in the document, the venture capitalist can come to the entrepreneur and ask to be bought out. If the entrepreneur can't come up with the money, the venture capitalist can then sell his share in the business to anyone he chooses.

While selling partial ownership in your business

can be risky, especially if you must turn to "un-friendly" sources, if you were ever to do it, this is the time. The entrepreneur with enough extra cash to buy or expand during this recession has the chance not to only improve his or her business in the short term but to position it for long-term success in the next decade.

CHAPTER 16

Renovating Your Home

To me every hour of the light and dark is a miracle,
Every cubic inch of space is a miracle.
—Walt Whitman

This recession is extremely frustrating for people who have outgrown their present homes. They're caught between fearful buyers, who keep waiting for real estate prices to drop farther, and stubborn sellers, who refuse to acknowledge that their homes have declined in value. Only a few short years ago I was advising young people to jump into home ownership as early as possible, even if it meant settling for a small "starter" home. In a few short years, I explained, they would be able to sell their first home and use the profit to step up to another, larger place. But the recession has changed all that.

Today in most of the country you can rarely sell your first home for a high enough price to be able to afford a new, larger one. And even if you can work your way out of this real estate sandwich, with home prices rising at most 5 percent annually, it takes three or more years just to recoup the transaction and moving costs. Those young people whom I urged to buy homes are now having children. Older clients of mine, who have been comfortable in their homes for years, are

now having to open up their nests for their parents or
for their grown children who can't afford housing of
their own. They're all coming to me asking for help in
breaking out of their real estate dilemmas.

I've been pointing out to them that there's a silver
lining hidden among all the clouds. The same forces
making it difficult to sell your current home and to buy
up are also dramatically cutting the costs of renovating
a home. With the real estate market stagnant, the construction trades and industries have no work. All
across the country architects, contractors, and lumberyards are desperate for business. They've never been
more willing to negotiate fees and prices.

That doesn't mean you should immediately put
down this book, get out the yellow pages, call the first
contractor you find list, and hire her to add two bedrooms onto your home. Home renovation is an expensive, time-consuming process with more than its share
of risks. Remember, you're altering your most important asset. Despite the current lull in real estate, the
home is still the foundation of personal wealth in
America. It can be used to finance new business ven-
tures, a child's college education, or retirement—so
anything that affects its value must be approached
carefully.

And despite what you might think, the cost of renovations isn't automatically added to the value of your
home. It may cost $40,000 to install a centralized
audio/video system, but the system probably adds only
$10,000 to your home's market value. So $30,000 of the
cost is sunk into the ground. In booming real estate
markets I see nothing wrong with spending some
money for an improved quality of life. But during a
recession, when real estate prices are tumbling, you
should look at renovations from as purely a financial
point of view as possible. Even if a renovation is de-

signed to forestall your need to move, eventually you'll want to sell your home. And then your life-style additions may come back to haunt you. I advise clients to limit luxury additions, if at all possible, to those things that always recoup their cost, such as fireplaces and skylights.

Real estate values are determined by the sales of comparable properties. Similar houses on a suburban block may vary in quality, but they'll all be priced within a 30 percent range. If the average price for houses in your area is $200,000, the most magnificent one on the block is worth no more than $230,000, and the worst is valued at no less than $170,000. No matter how extensively or how luxuriously you renovate your home, it never sells for more than the top end of its range. No one spends $300,000 for a home in a neighborhood where all the other houses sell for $200,000.

You'll recoup renovation costs by bringing your home up to the character of others in the area or by putting it in tip-top shape. In a neighborhood where the homes have either two or three bedrooms, the homeowner who adds a third bedroom to his two-bedroom home, or who spruces up his three-bedroom home, recoups his cost. A person who adds a fourth bedroom doesn't. That doesn't mean you shouldn't add the fourth bedroom if you're in desperate need of more space—just be aware that you may not get back the money you've invested.

Similarly stay away from below-ground or windowless additions. Another bedroom in a finished basement may suit your needs for more space, but it won't add to your home's value. Adding a wing or extension makes more sense financially. Even better are dormer and attic expansions, which cost less, since there's no need to excavate and extend the foundation. There's one caveat, however: Don't destroy the aesthetics of your home by building up or out. Buyers today value architectural consistency and details and shy away from any home that looks like it's a bunch of nondescript rooms just stuck together without rhyme or reason.

Modernizations and cosmetic renovations are also good values. Since they've come to realize real estate prices won't rise as rapidly as in the past, buyers are now trying to buy as big a home as they possibly can. Rather than purchasing a small home with the intent of selling it within five years and using the profit to buy another, larger home, buyers are stretching to buy a home they'll live in for a longer period of time—one they can grow into. Therefore they won't have fix-up money for quite some time. That's why modern kitchens and bathrooms are today bringing an added premium, as are recent overall paint jobs, sanded and finished floors, and new windows.

If you want a rough estimate of how much a potential renovation will add to the value of your home, speak with local real estate brokers or hire a real estate appraiser. For a fee of between $75 and $150 they should be willing to do an analysis of your home's projected value.

Once you've decided on the size and nature of the renovation, your next step should be to line up expert help. Regardless of how simple a project you have in mind, I recommend you get at least some professional assistance. If your renovation is strictly cosmetic and involves only one trade, you can hire a subcontractor directly. If your cosmetic project involves more than one trade, you should turn to a general contractor. And if your project is more than cosmetic, involving additions or modifications to the floor plan or footprint of the house, you should speak to a licensed architect.

It's obvious that an architect brings design skills

and aesthetic judgments to a renovation project, but it's just as important to get him or her to document the work to be done. In order to obtain accurate estimates from general contractors, every bidder must be working from the same information. That's easy when the job consists of simply replacing bathroom fixtures. But when it involves ripping down walls or adding rooms, it can be a problem. Contractors project their personal ideas onto projects that aren't documented with plans, which can lead to wide discrepancies in estimates.

A comprehensive set of plans also ensures that the project is finite. When a renovation is an organic process—constantly growing and changing—its price tag is organic as well. You'll never know exactly how much the work costs until just before it's finished.

Incomplete plans also leave an opening for unscrupulous contractors to take advantage of you. Some look for every opportunity to ask for additional money. They'll claim that the plans didn't specify that your windows had to open, so they'll add another few hundred dollars onto the bill. Rather than clarifying things with you up front, they'll wait for problems to crop up and try to capitalize on them.

Experienced local architects can also help ease the path through your building department or zoning board. Not only will they know what forms, if any, you need to file but in many cases their signature on an application means the form gets immediate approval. While the most common way to find an architect is through personal recommendations, when doing renovation work it makes sense to also contact your local building department for suggestions.

Once you've gotten a list of architects from friends and the building department, arrange to interview each. Concentrate on determining how much experience they have doing projects like yours. Look for evidence of professionalism and relevant experience. Try to determine if there's enough personal rapport between the two of you for the architect to be able to interpret your wants and needs and to translate them into concrete plans. A good architect is one who gives the client what the client wants. Finally check their references. While most architects want a percentage of the total cost of the job—generally 15 percent—try to get an hourly fee instead. This could range from $75 to $150, depending on the architect's reputation and experience. If you can't talk him into an hourly charge, get a cap on his fee.

Make sure your agreement with the architect clearly defines the nature of his services. In addition to consulting with you, preparing plans and designs, and coming up with price estimates, architects automatically include a project supervision fee. This involves verifying that the work is being done up to professional standards and in accordance with his plans. Sounds good at first, but since architects are trained to design, not to build, architectural supervision doesn't include checking into the contractor's hours, bookkeeping, or bills.

Occasional loose supervision by a homeowner is sufficient in small and midsized projects. Just being around, watching deliveries, and taking note of when work starts and stops should keep the contractors on their toes. Major renovations, however, require hands-on supervision because minor delays can result in thousands of dollars down the drain. Since your architect doesn't really have the knowledge or time needed to do the job right—remember, architectural education centers on design, not construction—another professional must be called in: a construction manager.

These individuals or firms are specialists in construction supervision. They're paid on a fee basis, depending upon the nature and scope of the project and the services required—either 3 to 5 percent of the total cost of the job or between $75 and $100 per hour—and serve as the owner's representative on the site, offering as much supervision as is necessary. The local building department can help you get some names, and your architect may have some recommendations.

Every multitrade renovation project requires a general contractor. While you may be able to figure out which subcontractors you'll need and then go out and hire them, only a general contractor has the knowledge and experience to coordinate and schedule their work. They also have more leverage with subcontractors than homeowners do, since they can provide a steady supply of work.

The best way to select a general contractor is to bring together a group of prescreened individuals and to ask them bid on your architect's plans. Prescreening is vital. Since there are no requirements for becoming a general contractor—all it takes is an advertisement and a pickup truck—the field has more than its share of crooks and con artists. Once again, you can prescreen by getting recommendations from your building department and architect. Don't worry about becoming too familiar to the folks down at city hall. Using architects and contractors who meet their approval is like taking out an insurance policy: You won't have any problem with them later on.

However, it's not enough insurance to keep you from having to check further. Select six of the recommended contractors and check with their references and the local Better Business Bureau. Ask each for their Social Security number and have your banker check their credit. Any contractor with poor credit has to pay a premium for materials and has the potential to go out of business before finishing your job. If some-one refuses to give you their Social Security number, they've got something to hide and should be scratched off your list.

Select three of the general contractors and present them with your architect's plans. I advise asking for a flat fee, or budget price—a guaranteed price based on the set of drawings—and avoiding fees based on time and materials—which gives the contractor a great deal of leeway and invariably results in time and cost over-runs. If they're hesitant to offer a flat fee, offer to share any potential savings with them, but insist that penalt-ies also be written into the contract. (Just bear in mind there could be surprises in store for both you and the contractor once walls are opened up.) Remember, they're desperate for work these days, so you've a great deal of leverage. Insist that the bids be broken down by the individual trades and that a materials list be included.

Compare the bids carefully. Try to figure out why the prices are different—rest assured, they will be. Pay particular attention to the bids of the individual sub-contractors. If one is overpriced you can always ask the general contractor to go back and get another price. Study the materials list provided by your bidders. In many cases, by paying cash up front a consumer can get a better price on raw materials and supplies than a contractor—lumberyards are as desperate for cash as the rest of us. Any bids that are way out of line indicate stupidity, desperation, lack of interest, or a complete misreading of the plans—none of which are good. If all the bids are well above your architect's estimate, the problem is with your plan. Ask the architect to prepare another, more realistic, set of plans as soon as possible.

While it's convenient if you like him or her, choos-ing a general contractor isn't a personality contest. The essential factors are that he or she be able to do the job well, within the time and budget agreed to. In order to guarantee that your job goes according to plan, you'll need an airtight contract. Don't sign the bidding forms many general contractors use as their agreement forms. Instead have your attorney draft an agreement. It should only take him or her between one and one-half to two and one-half hours. Your agreement should include the following:

- A discussion of all the financial terms, such as the total price, the down payment, and when further payments are to be made and in what amounts. Limit your down payment to 10 percent and tie other payments to the percentage of work completed.
- A statement that you'll be retaining 10 percent of each scheduled payment and turning the money over thirty days after the architect certifies that the project has been completed and that all necessary permits have been filed and accepted.
- A complete description of the work to be performed, along with a separate list of materials, a clause that allows you to buy materials on your own and reap the savings, and a schedule of prices for extra work (such as additional electrical outlets).
- An approximate starting date and completion date, as well as penalties for tardiness and rewards for promptness.
- A provision that all work be performed in a "good and workmanlike" manner and in accordance with all applicable building codes.
- A statement placing the responsibility for obtaining necessary permits and providing adequate insurance coverage squarely on the contractor.
- The terms and conditions of warranties on materials

and workmanship, including the names and addresses of the parties who will honor them.

• A clause stating that the contractor will devote full time to your job—hard to obtain, but worth fighting for.

• A provision that states that the contract cannot be assigned to another contractor, insuring the person you hire will be the person who does the job.

With the contract signed, all there is left to figure out is how you're going to pay for the work. If the job costs less than $3,000, it makes sense to pay cash and avoid interest and finance charges. Just make sure this doesn't cut into your six-month cash reserve.

If you project costs more than $3,000 but less than $10,000, your best bet is to take out a standard home improvement loan. These can be either secured or unsecured and run from five to seven years. Home improvement loans are easy to get, but their short terms and high interest rates translate into fairly steep monthly payments. An alternative is the Federal Housing Administration's Title I program, through which participating banks provide fifteen-year home improvement loans of up to $17,500. The loans, however, are restricted to what the government considers nonluxury projects. Bear in mind the interest on home improvement loans is tax deductible only if your home is used as collateral.

If your renovation costs more than $10,000, it makes sense to try to draw on the equity you've built up in your home. There are three ways you can do this: Obtain a home-equity loan; take out a home-equity line of credit; or refinance your mortgage. Your equity is equal to the difference between your home's current market value and the balance of your mortgage. If your home is worth $300,000 and you have $200,000 left to pay off, you have $100,000 worth of equity. However, you don't automatically qualify for a $100,000 home equity loan.

Bankers, in general, loan a maximum of 80 percent of total equity. However, they'll base the specific amount of each loan on the borrower's ability to meet the monthly payments. While you may have $100,000 in equity, if a banker believes you can only afford to pay back $40,000, that's all he'll loan. Some banks have special loan programs for valued customers that help maximize their borrowing ability. The bankers do this by basing their loan on what the home will be worth after the renovation is completed. Of course they won't give you the money until the work is done, requiring you to use their guarantee as collateral for another, short-term loan. Regardless of how much you borrow, the IRS only lets you deduct the interest from the first $100,000 of home equity debt.

Your equity borrowing can take the form of a standard home-equity loan or a home-equity line of credit. A loan gives you a lump-sum payment and anywhere from ten to thirty years to pay it back at interest rates generally fixed at one or two points above prime. Lines of credit let you draw money whenever you wish, either by writing a check or using a special credit card, and they charge interest only on the amount you spend. If you need to know exactly how much you'll be spending each month, take out a straight loan. Otherwise opt for a line of credit—it minimizes your interest charges.

Another way to draw on equity is to refinance your mortgage. Back in chapter 3 you'll find information on determining whether mortgage refinancing is worthwhile. Just be sure to check with your accountant first about how your tax status will be affected.

If you want to finance a major renovation but don't have enough equity to borrow against to pay for it, an alternative would be to take out an unsecured personal loan. While they're relatively easy and quick to obtain, the high rates of nondeductible interest and short terms lead to very high monthly payments. Normally I would say that these should be used only as a last resort after checking into every other alternative. But in a recession I advise you to stay clear of them entirely. While home renovation holds out the opportunity to improve your life-style in the short term, and your bank balance in the long term, it's still not a good enough reason to take on excessively painful debt during a recession when you're trying to conserve cash.

HOME RENOVATION FLOW CHART

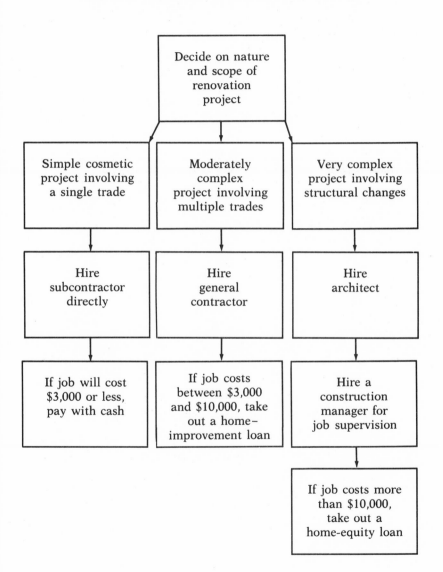

CHAPTER 17

Buying a Vacation or Weekend Home

We need the tonic of wildness. . . .
We can never have enough of nature.
—Henry David Thoreau

The contrary nature of a recession is nowhere more pronounced than in the recreational real estate market. Vacation areas are being harder hit by this recession than other parts of the country. While homes in suburbia may have dropped up to 20 percent in value, those in the vacation areas—such as Vail, Colorado; Nantucket, Massachusetts; and Hilton Head, South Carolina—have dropped more than 30 percent. The reason is that the always limited market for recreational real estate becomes even more limited in a recession.

Financially strapped Americans are cutting back on their luxury spending. That means that fewer people are renting vacation homes. Once the rental market starts drying up, those who own second homes find it difficult to carry the costs of ownership. Without rent defraying the cost of mortgage payments, taxes, and maintenance, owning a second home can become a financial drain. And if things weren't going so well to begin with, the costs of the second home can be the straw that threatens to break the camel's back. In re-

sponse owners of second homes put their places up for
sale. So what do we have? A recreational real estate
market in which there are fewer potential buyers than
ever before, and more anxious sellers than ever before.
That means there's an unprecedented opportunity to
buy prime vacation property.

I know what you're thinking: Weekend or vacation
homes are only for the wealthy. But thanks to the recession, real estate prices in second-home areas have
dropped to levels within the reach of middle-income
Americans. I believe owning a second home can be one
of the great pleasures of life. Aside from my wife and
children, my summer home on Martha's Vineyard
gives me the most joy. I'm not saying that if you
couldn't afford a second home before the recession, you
can today, or that you should stretch your income and
assets to the breaking point in order to buy. But if
prior to the recession you were thinking about buying
a summer home and, after setting aside your cash reserves and solidifying your finances you find you can
still afford it, go for it. If you were previously thinking
of buying in, let's say, a middle-income, lakefront community, today, for the same money, you can afford to
buy in an upper-income, oceanfront area.

But in order for you not to fall into the same trap
as those who are currently selling their second homes,
you must be a savvy buyer and realize the differences
between buying part-time and full-time homes. Your
timing, goals, affordability, priorities, and financing
are all different.

Although I am so enamored of the second home as
a source of life enhancement that I urge my clients to
buy one as early in their lives as they can, it's possible
to buy too soon. If you overburden your stream of income with the costs of a second home too soon, you'll
dilute your ability to buy a new full-time home. I don't

think you're ready to buy a second home until you've spent at least four years in the home you intend to keep until your children leave the nest or you retire. At that point your income has probably grown into your mortgage payments and you'll start feeling comfortable enough to take on additional debt.

It's a mistake to buy a second home thinking it's a good investment. Buy for pleasure, not for profit. If you buy something you love, you'll use it regularly and hold on to it for a very long time. By default, then, it will have grown in value and become a sound investment. If, on the other hand, you buy with the intent of using it occasionally, renting it to recoup costs, and then selling in a few years for a profit, you're taking a big risk. The property has stopped being a second home and become an investment property, subject to all the fluctuations of the market. And as you can see all around you today, recreation areas are very volatile. In bad times they suffer more, and even in times of general economic prosperity they can be erratic. Vacation rental markets go up and down depending on what's "hot" or "chic" that particular season. The tax advantages of being able to depreciate your second home pale in comparison with the aggravations of having to pander to summer or weekend renters—who tend to be prima donnas—and the possible market fluctuations.

If you buy your second home as a life enhancer, not an income or profit producer, you won't need to worry about market fluctuations and changing tastes. Sure, I'm somewhat concerned about the fact that my home in Martha's Vineyard has dropped about 30 percent in value—I wouldn't be human if I wasn't. But I bought it for the pleasure it would bring my family and me. It gives us the opportunity to take frequent, inexpensive, minivacations all year long. Martha's

Vineyard has been a constant in my family for more than twenty years now, and will remain so for the rest of my life. If sometime, way off in the future, the house is sold and brings a handsome profit, that's icing on the cake.

Calculating how much you can afford to spend on a second home is very similar to figuring out how much you could spend on your first home. It's a matter of adding up all the things you'll be willing to give up in exchange. First, take a careful look at how much you and all your family members spend each year on vacations. Include the costs of travel, hotels, meals, gifts, and any new clothes you would buy for a trip. And make sure you include those little weekend getaways as well as your two-week summer vacation. All of this money can be funneled into the purchase of a second home. Examine all your other "luxury" expenses carefully. Are you willing to forgo new living room furniture this year, a new wardrobe every season, a movie or restaurant meal a week, a play or concert a month?

You don't need to limit yourself to luxury sacrifices. While obviously you shouldn't let the purchase of a second home inhibit your ability to pay for your first home, or impact on your child's education fund or your six-month cash reserve, it might make sense to draw from retirement funds. Your summer home could become your retirement home in later years. When you do retire, you'll already have your shelter lined up, so whatever proceeds you get from the sale of your full-time home can be invested and used for living expenses.

Even though it might sound like a good idea at first, don't buy a second home in partnership with friends. Your relationship may be solid today, but there's no telling what could happen in the future—especially when it's placed under the strain of being housemates and business partners as well as friends. All buying decisions become compromises. That all but ensures that one or both becomes unhappy—probably sooner rather than later. At that point there's either a buyout or a mutual sale. And when the second-home partnership ends, so, probably, does the friendship.

I made the mistake of buying my first home on Martha's Vineyard in partnership with a friend. Things went well for about three years, but then my friend and his family got bored with the house. They wanted to sell and vacation somewhere else. My family and I, however, loved the Vineyard and didn't want to give it up. I scraped together as much money as I could and negotiated a way to buy my partner out. Needless to say, my family didn't lose the house. However, I lost the friendship.

Your priorities are different when looking for a second home. Location is vital in the selection of any real estate, but with a vacation home it's doubly vital. The purpose of this home is pleasure and relaxation, so the environment must be beautiful and serene. That's why, while you pay a premium for proximity to water—whether it's a lake, a stream, or the ocean—I think it's worth it.

Since you're cutting back on a large portion of your regular entertainment spending in order to afford this home, accessibility is important. My suggestion is you look at second homes that are more than one hundred, but less than three hundred miles from your full-time home. That way you'll get the best of both worlds: It's far enough away to be affordable yet near enough to get to for a weekend. Once you go more than two hours outside a major city, prices drop about 25 percent.

Try to limit your search to communities consisting primarily of second homes. You don't want to be forced to keep your part-time home up to the standards of neighbors for whom it's a full-time home. Make sure, however, there are goods, services, and tradespeople available year-round.

Look for a utilitarian house. You won't be entertaining formally in this house, so there's no need to impress anyone. It should have just enough amenities and space for you and your family. The common areas of a second home—kitchen and living room—are more important than the private areas—bedrooms and bathrooms. And any outside living areas, such as a patio or deck, are more of a plus than they would be in a full-time home. Low maintenance and ease of cleaning are priorities. You don't want to spend large parts of your vacation cleaning or fixing up the house. This home should be an escape from the burdens of everyday life, not a reminder of them. Make sure the house is, or can be, fully insulated. Otherwise its usefulness is limited to one or two seasons of the year.

Financing the purchase of a second home also requires a shift in approach. Most bankers in major metropolitan areas are hesitant to issue mortgages on second homes. They believe you're more likely to default on a second-home mortgage than on a first, since it's a luxury rather than a necessity, and they're afraid you'll be overextending yourself by taking on added debt. There's no sense trying to convince them they're wrong. These attitudes seem to become ingrained in someone the moment he or she becomes a banker. Instead look to small, local banks in the very area you're buying for second-home mortgages. Since the local economy and their business are directly tied to the second-home market, they'll be eager to help out qualified borrowers. If you can't obtain a mortgage from a local banker, consider using the equity you've built up in your full-time home to finance the purchase of a second home.

Finally, with the recreational real estate market in such bad shape, I think it's become a sine qua non for buyers of second homes to get the seller to take back paper. Rather than you coming up with a down payment, ask the seller to provide the money and in exchange give him or her a five-year non-interest-bearing note for the amount. (For more information on how to negotiate this type of deal, see chapter 18.) There's desperation out there among sellers of second homes, and savvy buyers can take advantage of it.

Second-Home Checklist

1. Buy for pleasure, not for profit.
2. Don't buy in partnership with another family.
3. Scenic location is a must.
4. You'll get the best price if more than one hundred miles from your year-round home, but make sure it's within three hundred miles so that it's accessible for weekend use.
5. Community should consist primarily of second-home owners.
6. Year-round services should be available.
7. Common spaces more important than private spaces.
8. Low maintenance is a priority.
9. Outdoor living areas and full insulation are bonuses.
10. Arrange financing with a bank in the same area.

CHAPTER 18

Buying Undeveloped Real Estate

It is a comfortable feeling to know that you stand on your own ground.
Land is about the only thing that can't fly away.
—Anthony Trollope

Whenever the economy takes a nosedive, a tremendous amount of vacant land goes up for sale. The market value of undeveloped real estate is, in the short term, extremely volatile. It's directly linked to the economic health of its surrounding area, and with most of the nation suffering, prices have dropped as much as 30 percent. Seeing the market value of their property fall to 1980 levels (adjusted for inflation) was the last straw for many people. Angered by declining value, and in search of increased liquidity, they've decided to trade in their long-term visions of real estate–generated profits for some good old-fashioned short-term cash in the bank. That makes 1991 a great time to buy raw land.

There's something thrilling about owning real estate. You stand on it and truly feel like you're worth something. It's an investment that's tangible and solid. And today it's affordable as well. Visions of a dream

home come to your mind. Or if you're a more entrepreneurial soul, perhaps you envision split levels popping
up everywhere. You find yourself repeating tales of
how some of the nation's wealthiest people started off
in the business of buying and selling land. Success is
certain, you believe. After all, God has stopped making
land but continues to make people.

But before you jump into the currently depressed
market and gobble up some raw land, it's essential
that you understand that buying undeveloped real estate is extremely complicated. Land values are very
subjective. Every piece of property is entirely unique,
so there's often no comparable parcel you can turn to
for an estimate of value. Instead value is determined
by potential productivity. That means that the price
you pay is based on your own judgment rather than on
the wisdom of the marketplace. In addition not every
parcel of raw land grows in value or can be built on.
There's property that will never be developed, no matter how long you wait nor how much the population
grows. And when a piece of raw land *does* go up in
value, the increase occurs over a very long period of
time. Meanwhile as you're waiting for it to go up in
value, or to accumulate the funds to build on it, your
costs—particularly taxes—increase with frightening
regularity.

And as if the process weren't complex enough, the
land business is filled with shady operators looking to
bilk unsuspecting consumers. Passing themselves off as
desperate to sell because of some recession-related
problem, these con artists often sell desolate, valueless
pieces of land. A few artist's renderings, a sign or two,
a colorful brochure, and some creative use of language—such as calling ten acres in the desert a ranch-
ette—are often enough to fool naive consumers.

Don't get me wrong. All these cautions notwithstanding, I still think the recession presents an exceptional opportunity to buy raw land—I just want you to buy it for the right reason. Even in the best of times I steer my clients away from buying land as an investment. And now with the economy in a recession, I'm more adamant in my opposition to it. Having been in the real estate business myself, I know how risky it can be. Even savvy professionals make mistakes—as I did. It's also the longest-term investment around. If you buy well and the property enters the development pipeline, you'll still be forced to wait an absolute minimum of five years to make a profit. And in order for the reward to justify the risk, you'll need to wait at least ten years. That's why I believe real estate speculation should be left to professionals.

However, I urge anyone who can afford it to use this recession as an opportunity to buy undeveloped land for his or her own use. That's a much simpler and safer process, since you don't need to worry about *if* the property will ever be developed. In effect you're the developer. All you need worry about is whether or not the property *can* be developed. If you're buying the land to keep someone else from using it—protecting your view or privacy—you don't even need to worry about that. Once you build your weekend, vacation, or dream home on the land, or add the parcel to your current tract, it moves from the volatile raw land market into the more stable home market. Even if you don't think you'll be able to build your dream home for another five to ten years, now is the time to buy the land it will sit on.

Let's go over the less common but simpler process of defensive land buying first. The secret here is to hire a representative and an adviser.

It's in your best interest to prevent the seller from finding out it's his or her neighbor who's interested in buying. That's because the property in question is worth more to you than it would be to someone else. For example, there may be hundreds of empty two-acre lots in your area, but there's only one that sits between your summer house and the lakefront. If the seller realizes the property holds unique value to you, his price rises dramatically. To keep that from happening, use a specialist real estate attorney to approach the seller or his broker and negotiate the deal. The first time the seller learns you're the buyer should be when he sees your signature on the contract. Generally, specialized real estate attorneys charge anywhere from $200 to $300 per hour.

You'll also need an experienced local real estate broker to help determine exactly how much you should pay for the land. Let's go back to the two-acre lot sitting between your summer house and the lakefront. Its market value may be about $150,000—but its value to you is different. What you need to determine is how much those two acres add to the value of your house. That requires some fairly sophisticated appraisal work on the broker's part, for which you should be willing to pay a broker's fee. If adding the two acres and ensuring uninterrupted view and access to the lake adds more than $150,000 to the value of your home, buying the property makes sense. While you don't want to pay more than the property's market value, realizing that it holds added value for you may justify being slightly less hardheaded during the negotiation.

Two years ago I bought a home in Connecticut. The property originally consisted of both a main house and a gate house. Despite my best efforts the seller decided to sell the two homes separately, believing he could get more for his money. I purchased the main house, but the gate house remained unsold for another year. At that time I contacted an experienced local broker and discovered that since the seller's price had dropped, I would now be able to buy the gate house for less than it would add to the value of the main property.

Buying property to actually build on is a bit more complicated. First, put down the real estate section of the newspaper and throw away all the brochures you sent away for: The secret is to buy the land rather than have it sold to you.

Start by pinpointing a general area of interest. While aesthetic beauty is important—you'll probably be holding on to this property for most of your life—it's not everything. If you intend to use this land for weekends, at least until you retire, it should be within a four-hour drive of your current home. Take out a map and with a compass, draw a circle with a radius of three hundred miles around your present home. If you ever intend this home to serve as a year-round residence, eliminate areas that are desolate or seasonally oriented. Exclude areas that are more than one hour's drive from an airport or a major highway. Of the areas that remain, circle those that are near water or mountains. Now get in your car and start investigating.

Once you've found a particular location you like, start nosing around. You're looking for land that isn't being actively marketed by a developer, so that means doing some digging. Speak to local real estate brokers—both residential and commercial—and local bankers. Tell them you're interested in relocating to the area and are looking for land to build a home on.

If you happen to fall in love with land that's in a developer's hands, you can often protect yourself somewhat by checking with the Interstate Land Sales Registration Division of the Department of Housing and Urban Development. Developers who operate across state lines and are selling more than one hundred lots must file disclosure statements with them. In addition they'll be able to tell you if there have been any complaints registered against the developer. You can check on the reputations of small local developers by calling the local office of the state attorney general, the state's consumer protection department or agency, and the local Better Business Bureau.

When you find a parcel that looks interesting, take a drive to the land. For a complete land-buying checklist, see pages 270 to 271. Make sure there's adequate access to the property. If the plot is landlocked with no road abutting it, scratch it off your list. If access consists of a private road, find out who's responsible for maintenance and what charges are involved. Try to walk the entire property. Bring a notebook and pen along with you on the hike for note taking.

If there's refuse dumped on the site, beware. While it may not indicate an environmental problem, it does mean there's regular trespassing.

Pay careful attention to tree roots and rock formations—both are clues to how expensive it will be to build on the site. When roots run close to or above the surface, it means the soil is either rocky or has a heavy clay content. Rock outcroppings are like icebergs—most of the problem is hidden below the surface. In both cases excavation and subsequent construction could be very expensive.

Watch out for signs of potential flooding problems. If the parcel is lower than the surrounding land, you may end up building your dream home in a swamp. Land that's high and dry is always the best buy.

Make sure you can identify the exact boundaries of the property. Don't assume the babbling brook, birch grove, or wonderful stone wall is actually part of your lot.

If the property is surrounded by other empty lots, always assume the worst. Never depend on the surrounding land remaining empty or being used in accordance with your wishes. If you love the view and it cuts across another lot, you must buy that lot as well to ensure your sight line.

On the other hand, if you find yourself looking at an empty lot in an otherwise built-up area, you should also be very careful. Since the natural laws of capitalism should have resulted in the land being developed, you can assume it's somehow diseased.

When you finish your walking tour, head back to your hotel room. Call the local utility and telephone companies and ask whether service can readily be brought to the property. Next contact the local office of the Environmental Protection Agency and find out if they have any evidence of problems with the particular lot you're interested in or those in the immediate vicinity. Finally telephone the local planning department or zoning board and ask if there are any restrictions on your use of the property.

The two big dangers you're looking to avoid are a "wetlands" classification and the presence of hazardous chemicals. The federal government's Clean Water Act defines a wetland as land that's sometimes wet or swampy and/or that supports certain varieties of animal and plant life. Land so classified cannot be built on without permission from the Army Corps of Engineers. Just because the property you're looking at is high and dry doesn't mean it's exempt. Sometimes even seasonal flooding or spot vegetation can result in a wetlands classification.

Another federal regulation, the 1980 Superfund Law, requires the owner of property contaminated by hazardous waste to pay for the cleanup, whether or not he created the problem. You could be responsible for cleaning up chemicals that were dumped on the land before you were even born.

If you get this far without finding a problem, it's time to get serious and send your professional team into action. Have your attorney commission a thorough title search and get her to double-check your own preliminary conversations with local officials and agencies. Ask her to recommend real estate appraisers and inspectors experienced with raw land. Select an appraiser and obtain a formal appraisal of the property's worth. Choose an inspector and arrange for a thorough investigation of the property's environmental conditions. Make sure the land is tested for its ability to support a cesspool system, and for the presence of radon—a carcinogenic gas that can be emitted by underground rock structures and absorbed into a home. Ask the inspector to recommend a well-digging contractor to provide an estimate of how much it will cost to provide an adequate supply of water.

Once you're satisfied that there's nothing wrong with the parcel, negotiations can start. Don't become fixated on the price tag of the land. The terms of the deal are actually much more important. Let me explain: Banks won't loan money to buy raw land unless there's a large down payment and sufficient collateral—usually a home. And even then they may balk. The only alternative to paying cash is to get the seller to take back paper. Serious sellers realize this and are generally willing to work out a mutually beneficial arrangement.

My suggestion is you that pursue a ten-year non-amortizing, nonrecourse (if possible) mortgage. You agree to pay the seller, monthly or semiannually, only the interest on the loan. At the end of ten years you owe the face value of the loan. *Nonrecourse* means you don't sign a note for the amount of the loan. If you default, the seller simply gets to take back ownership of the land. For example: on a $100,000, 10 percent mortgage, you would pay the seller $2,500 each quarter. At the end of ten years you would still owe him a one-time payment of $100,000. Hopefully at that time you'll be ready to build and can obtain enough construction financing to cover the $100,000 as well as your building costs. If you're not ready to build yet, you can either get the seller to refinance, sell the property to someone else, or arrange for alternative bank financing. You could even choose to walk away from the deal and let the seller take the land back, since you wouldn't be liable for any further payment.

This type of deal works out well for both parties: It gives sellers what they're looking for—a solid, guaranteed, cash return on an investment that otherwise was buried in the ground; and it gives you the chance to lock in today's low price for raw land and then pay for it with tomorrow's less-valuable dollars. If you do nothing else during this recession, it will still qualify as a success.

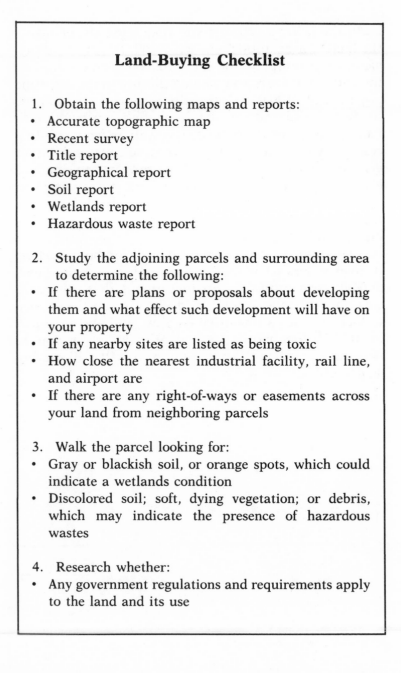

Land-Buying Checklist

1. Obtain the following maps and reports:
*   Accurate topographic map
*   Recent survey
*   Title report
*   Geographical report
*   Soil report
*   Wetlands report
*   Hazardous waste report

2. Study the adjoining parcels and surrounding area to determine the following:
*   If there are plans or proposals about developing them and what effect such development will have on your property
*   If any nearby sites are listed as being toxic
*   How close the nearest industrial facility, rail line, and airport are
*   If there are any right-of-ways or easements across your land from neighboring parcels

3. Walk the parcel looking for:
*   Gray or blackish soil, or orange spots, which could indicate a wetlands condition
*   Discolored soil; soft, dying vegetation; or debris, which may indicate the presence of hazardous wastes

4. Research whether:
*   Any government regulations and requirements apply to the land and its use

- Permits are required to build on the land and how long it takes to obtain them
- Engineers consider it "buildable"

5. Investigate if the following services are readily available:
- Telephone
- Utilities
- Water
- Garbage collection
- Road maintenance
- Fire and police protection
- Public schools
- Sewage hookups